Awakening to the Obvious

Adyashakti

Awakening to the Obvious
By Adyashakti 1952

—

© 2013 Equanimity Books
All rights reserved.
ISBN: 10:1493599666
ISBN: 13:978-1493599660

Contents

Introduction

In January, 1994, after a contemplative practice of more than two decades, I awoke to the transcendent heart. That fact, plus a couple bucks, entitles me to a (small) cup of Starbuck's coffee. I've waited nearly 20 years to publish these essays about my experience of awakening—in order to give the stink of enlightenment time to wear off.

My penname, Adyashakti, is Sanskrit for "Primordial Energy." I'm a former national magazine editor, and an award-winning author of several novels, one of them published in 10 languages. I'm married (for more than a quarter century), with two grown sons, a grizzled old greyhound, and a nearly paid-off mortgage. I spent my twenties and thirties studying the world's religions, with particular focus on the mystics of each faith; in my forties I wrote science fiction; in my fifties I spent seven years teaching world religions at the university level. I'm 61 as I write this book.

I am not a guru, lama, roshi, or spiritual master, nor any kind of "purified" or "perfected" human being. (Just ask my wife or kids. Or dog.) I am not living in a special state of grace, nor undergoing unusual experiences, nor do I possess supernormal abilities. Indeed, without wearing glasses, I would not even be able to clearly see these words as I type.

In short, nothing about me as a personality could be called extraordinary. Yet this does not detract from the matter at hand: I do understand my original nature, as described in Buddhist and other mystical teachings of the past twenty-five centuries. I have seen beyond the limits of conventional identity, into the open nature (free capacity) of consciousness itself.[1]

Therefore, it is clear to me that enlightenment (or the enjoyment of reality) is not opposed to the flow of ordinary life and change and death; not at odds with car payments, health insurance premiums, and the lifestyle of a modern Western householder.

The standard notion of wisdom is that it consists of a body of knowledge and methods that one can memorize and then stridently practice. This book is not about that kind of wisdom; it offers no special doctrine the reader can adhere to. "The Great Way has no back," said the Chinese sage Lao Tzu. "Thus, it cannot be followed." Reading the essays herein won't gain for you esoteric information and new techniques for manipulating body, mind and world. However, this book may help you to reconcile with the inherent mystery of life *as it is*, and thus be one with (no longer at odds with) the Great Way.

Like the taste of fresh, clear water, "enlightenment" is subtle to describe. Yet it is here for the tasting, and even the most carefully chosen words become obsolete as soon as you take the first sip.

---

[1] Such awakening is considered the "middle" of the journey of enlightenment. The path begins with inquiry, consideration and contemplation. Gradually or suddenly, awakening dawns; then follows the integration and personalization of enlightenment in everyday experience, maturing throughout one's lifetime.

The power of this book will be in your own response—or not. It will touch you where you live—or not. No praise, no blame. For those with whom it resonates, may this book help you to taste deeply your own open and luminous, original nature.

ADYASHAKTI

Foreword

How can one communicate in written language the
"Open Secret"—the *awakeness* of those who are
awake? The more deeply one intuits and feels the
essential mystery, the more words are stripped away
until one is left as speechless as a newborn.
Therefore, in writing this book I'm behaving like Lao
Tzu, the ancient Chinese mystic, who claimed that,
"He who knows does not speak; he who speaks does
not know"—and who then proceeded to write 81
verses on the subject of his divine ignorance.

The problem, of course, is the gaping
difference between direct experience and verbal
description. Look up in a dictionary the word
"orgasm" and it does not make your heart beat like a
conga. Timothy Leary once said in a different
context: "For those who have had the experience, no
words are necessary. For those who have not had the
experience, no words are possible."

Lao Tzu again: "The Way that can be told is
not the Great Way." True enough; the infinitude of
reality can never be reduced to words. So maybe I
should just shut up and let the Tao flow on in
profound silence. No words, no misstatements.

On the other hand, I know that in spite of
Lao Tzu's paradoxical warning, many people
(including myself) have received useful, graceful

wisdom from his teachings, twenty-five centuries after he set calligraphy brush to silk.[2]

Indeed, I have come to understand the same wonderful truth about which Lao Tzu reluctantly (yet so eloquently) writes—the original nature of all persons and things—and I can't seem to help myself from trying to communicate this insight to my friends.

Admittedly, words are clumsy and fragmenting, whereas the Tao is subtle and seamlessly whole. Trying to tell the Way in words is like trying to paint a tiny scene on a grain of rice using a barn brush. But like Lao Tzu, aware of my own foolishness, I'm going to be as plainspoken as I can be about the unsayable.

---

[2] Most scholars do not believe Lao Tzu ("Old Man") was an actual historical figure, so here I am speaking poetically.

My Awakening to the Obvious

1972

When I was nineteen, I was blessed with a wonderful mystical vision: I experienced the light of God. That is, I experienced what Tibetan Buddhists call *Osel* (or "Primordial Clear Light"), and Hindu yogis describe as *Sahasradala Padma* ("Thousand-Petal Lotus of Light"). Chinese Taoists call it *Ming* ("Transcendent Luminosity"). Sioux Indians name it *Wakan Tonka* ("Great Spirit"). Muslims refer to it as *Noor* ("Divine Resplendence"). It is also *Kavod* ("Eternal Flame") that shines at the altar of Judaism; the same radiance of which Jesus said, "If your eye is single, your whole body will be filled with light."

The word *light* is not used here as a figure of speech (symbolizing a brighter, sunnier, higher aspect of ourselves and the cosmos). All these names and images refer to <u>actual</u> light: self-luminous, all-pervading energy. It is *the* living force—radiant consciousness—ablaze with bliss. Communion with this holy light, absorption in it is unspeakably pleasurable. Yet in my case, the event of drowning in the ocean of brightness left a great disturbance in its wake that took decades to resolve.

Let me tell you my story.

In 1972 I was a sophomore at Boston University, a teen-age son of 20th-century America, who listened to Led Zeppelin cranked up loud enough to vibrate my teeth. I was not exactly preparing body and mind for a direct encounter with the divine. My Jewish religious training had consisted of attending Sabbath services and Sunday school as a boy, which felt like sitting for several hours a week in front of an unplugged radio. Until the age of about nine, I had believed in and prayed to the Judeo-Christian Deity, but by the time I was ten or so, I began to aggressively disbelieve in an anthropomorphic Father-God. Natural science and science fiction became far more inspiring, meaningful and beautiful to me than conventional religious dogma. At age eleven, I had quit attending the synagogue.

Even so, there was a mystical streak in me that I had noticed from my earliest memories. It showed itself as a keenly felt sense of the mystery of the natural world and human life. This feeling of wonder or awe would sometimes rise in me as a bodily thrill until I had to laugh or shout.

1971 As a college freshman I took a world religions course because I intuited something fundamental to the religious urge in people, something prior to arguing over the different notions of God, something primitive, below the abstract verbal mind that has created all the historical schisms of exoteric beliefs. I wanted to find this most basic truth at the root of all faiths. I longed to be like a lover—a naked beginner in the embrace of Living Nature. I personally wanted to know "It"—the real God—for I somehow understood "It" to be the depth and ground of my own heart. Thus, I sought contact with my deepest heart, from which I was seemingly in exile.

1972 The next year, as a sophomore, I took an excellent class on Eastern philosophy. We read the *Heart Sutra* of Buddha and essays on Zen by D.T. Suzuki; *Psychotherapy East and West*, by Alan Watts and *Modern Man in Search of a Soul*, by Carl Jung; the principal *Upanishads* and the *Bhagavad Gita* of the Hindus; the *Tao Teh Ching* of Lao Tzu; the *Yoga Sutras* of Patanjali. I began to have grand insights into my own condition, though I understood only a fraction of what I read.

Then some classmates invited me to their apartment for a dinner discussion of the profound teachings we were studying. Steve had been a Theravada Buddhist monk in Thailand for two years, meditating seventeen hours a day; John was an avid student of yoga and Vedanta; and Sean had deserted the French Army and walked through India for three years, meeting holy persons. In contrast, I had neither meditated, nor done yoga, nor spent time in the company of anyone who was especially wise and free.

After dinner, riding the crest of the moment, everyone but Sean took LSD together. It was my sixth psychedelic trip. We took turns reading aloud from the Old Testament's *Genesis* and from *Be Here Now*, a primer on Hindu mysticism. After a while, Steve read to us from *The Psychedelic Experience*, a "trip manual" by Timothy Leary and Ralph Metzner, based on the *Tibetan Book of the Great Liberation* (also called *Tibetan Book of the Dead*).

Early on in the six-hour LSD high, I began to feel the same deep awe that I'd enjoyed as a boy, only stronger now than ever. The emotion seemed to expand and fill body, mind and room as a tangible presence: a sphere of invincible energy and happiness. I was sitting on a ratty carpet on the living room floor of a cheap apartment in Cambridge, immersed in a force field of great joy. I looked at Steve with drunken love and said, "The Holy Spirit is upon us."

But I began to notice an apparent limit to the spirit, like a knot or cramp within the otherwise boundless force and presence. It gradually became obvious that the knot was "me"—or everything I held onto as "myself". I saw that the whole melodrama of "me" (as a separated or independent and limited identity) was based on this unconscious habit of <u>withholding</u> (contracting, recoiling from whole and infinite being). "Me" was only a construct, not ultimately real (not a real entity or identity), but merely an *act* (like a fictional stage character) within Free and Total Being. And mistakenly (ridiculously!), the sense of identity had been bound to this mere role, this temporary personality, this psycho-physical ego (as if Life and Consciousness were an isolated self that is born to change and die). Such phony (separate) identity was the cause of all fear—the refusal to love and shine completely; the resistance to change and death, and thus, to all of life and relationship.

Within Consciousness, the dream of "me" was suddenly released. In that instant, came the deep heart of understanding: The <u>totality</u> of conscious being is the real and living "Person", the all-inclusive Identity of everyone and everything. As the sages have put it, "There is *only* God."

I fell onto my back in tears with the overwhelming relief of this realization of transcendental (unlimited) life. I surrendered utterly to my felt-intuition of the Great One. Rapidly, a marvelous change occurred. Layers of subtler self-holding fell away and I melted into the heart of God. I did not just watch this self-transcendence occur, as if from the bleachers. Ego-"I" *dissolved* in the all-effacing light of Existence-Consciousness-Bliss.

To the extent the experience can be described, it was something like this: In the first few seconds of self-surrender, a glorious golden light filled mind and body and all of space. Mind (or attention) was captured by the light and drawn

10

inward and upward toward an infinite locus above. Outer awareness disappeared as attention, body and world were resolved into the unity of the light-source—like an iris blossom refolding and returning to its bud. Just at the brink of ego-death there was an instant of fear, but I knew there was no turning back, no stopping this expansion beyond all limit. And I knew that whatever this sacrifice led to, it simply was Reality.

Therefore, I silently prayed, "Have mercy on me," and in the next instant the light became so supremely attractive it absorbed the fear along with everything else into its dazzling singularity. As the last bit of self-hold evaporated, the golden light increased to "white," or rather, it became perfectly *clear, pure, unqualified, original.* There was no more expansion, no more ascent; indeed there was no more "up" or "down," "in" or "out," but all of existence was radically equal and whole—the same absolutely bright fullness (or emptiness).

I was conscious as limitless radiant being, identical with the Self or Source of the universe. I don't know how long I remained consumed in that domain of ecstasy, but it was *utterly familiar*, not new or shocking. It was Home, eternally. That Which *IS* (or the One *I AM*).

Of course, I came down. With a splat!

Crashed, as they say; and back again from the ego-centered point of view of a white, middle-class American kid who had grasped only a fraction of what he had read from the Oriental mystics, the experience of the light was not only incomprehensible, it was terrifying. By the following afternoon, I felt so upset, I was pale and shaky. After all, what was so attractive about the dissolution of ego, the death of "me"? I had developed a painful case of psychic indigestion.

At first I tried to resist the revelation of the light, the divine intrusion on my independent, private life. I wanted to say, "Go away, I'm not ready for this. I just want to be me. I want to stay me."

Lost and scared, I compulsively tried to secure the threatened ego, reinforce its boundaries and make it solid, immune to change. It didn't work. There is no way to go on as an isolated self once you've tumbled into the heart of infinite life, even if only for a timeless instant. (As the Muslim poet Kabir said, "I saw that for thirty seconds, and it has made me a devotee all my life.")

WHEN ALL ELSE FAILS, READ THE DIRECTIONS.

I did.

I began to study the teachings of the Eastern and Western mystics in earnest. (It is noteworthy that all of them warn not to delve into mystical experience without proper preparation and a guide who knows the territory.)

It took time, more than a decade, but gradually my anxiety and confusion waned and was replaced by a growing understanding. Along the way I discovered scores of historical sources in which ego-loss in the radiant, transcendental being is described. Classical yoga provides a Sanskrit term for the experience: *nirvikalpa samadhi.* [3]Many teachers quickened my awakening; not the least among them my wife and our two sons.

This does not mean I fitted the revelation of the divine to my everyday life—like pocketing a shiny new coin and then continuing on my private

---

[3] Translation: *sam* ("total") *adhi* ("total absorption") *nir* ("without") *vikalpa* ("mental formations"). It describes the trance state of complete absorption in consciousness itself, without the appearance of any sensory or mental object.

way. No. The divine is senior to self and world and will not be owned. Therefore, I did the reverse: I submitted my life to the divine; I became a devotee of God. Not the Almighty Absent Parent who never speaks through the dead radio, but the same wonderful, living Source and starry Process that a naturalist can love with awe.

Also, I began to meditate. I practiced a simple technique of focusing on the in and out of *1987* my breath while sitting quietly. After fifteen years of this simple practice, I experienced a "return" to the light. While deeply in tune with the breath, my attention spontaneously became focused in the mid-brain, between and behind the eyes. Thus my "eye" became "single." My whole body was filled with light, as Jesus promised. I sat in a swoon and received the golden light into all my parts. At the time, I wrote an essay proclaiming: "Holy light is not a metaphor. Dazzlingly alive is the eternal spirit."

But I was still afraid.

I was afraid of madness—the utter sacrifice of self and all limit. No knowing. No controlling. No "me." I was afraid of drowning in infinity.

Six years later, in February 1993, a turning point arrived. I stood on my balcony in a contemplative mood, feeling into life, and I recalled a line a friend had told me years before about "meeting God halfway." That notion now seemed absurd, as I saw that God Is Here, already *all the way present.* Nothing is hidden or withheld. I said aloud a motto that summed this up: "The gift is always given." It was a beautiful, religious sense of being lived and loved and breathed by God.

Suddenly, a tremendous Force pressed down from above my head, through my brain and nervous system, with such mighty light and bliss that I fell to my knees and was pinned, overwhelmed bodily by the tangible brightness, as one might be overwhelmed by a terribly powerful orgasm. I gasped and sobbed from the potency of the joy. The God-pleasure—the saturating fullness and Touch of the light—became so intense I felt my bones might crack.

When I stood up, I had changed physically.

And my meditations changed. For several years, I'd been aware of powerful, "electrical" surges in my nervous system during meditation. I had focused on the breath and ignored these stirrings of the *kundalini*.[4] But now my meditation sessions became sheer energy work-outs. Even so simple a practice as following the breath now felt like contrived self-effort. My method of meditation had been rendered obsolete. Instead, I would sit and the kundalini would flame through my head and eyes and spine and toss me around like a mad dancer. I laughed and cried. I growled. I shouted. I made spontaneous chant-like intonations. I saw archetypal visions.[5]

It was painful and blissful—indescribable. I was suffering, but unable to budge a finger; afraid,

---

[4] *Kundalini* and *Kundalini Shakti* are Sanskrit terms for the primordial life-force or universal energy as it functions in the human body-mind. The closest Western term would be Holy Spirit. The arousal and release of this latent power in the course of meditation or devotional prayer, etc., is what Western mystics call "spiritual baptism."

[5] An oft-recurring vision was of the hexangular "Star of David" of Judaism, which is also a common symbol in Hindu and Buddhist Tantra. The upward- and downward-pointing interpenetrating triangles, formed of brilliant light, stood in space before my inner eye, with my seated form (in lotus-posture) fitting inside the mandala star. I understood bodily that this archetype expresses the harmonized fullness of the ascending and descending currents of the life-force (*kundalini shakti*).

but unable to make a single response. I was being meditated.

I became constantly aware of the tension around my heart, the tension of "me"—of holding on to myself. The presence of spirit had become a great current and my misery was my resistance to it. But I was reluctant to sacrifice "my life" completely.

Eight months later, in October 1993, I had grown so exhausted with the effort of preventing my own death, that I lay down on my bed and said, *Okay, I give up. Take me insanity, or take me God, or take me whatever you are, mighty river. Sweep me to my destiny.*

Abruptly, I began to lose "face." Panic came on strong. I cramped up in a ball like a fetus. I became an electric buzzing cloud and then everything dissolved and I entered the light and bliss and freedom of ego-death; beyond the golden light into the clear light of void. No self. No thing. No bounds. The rapture only lasted a few seconds, but it was enough to see that all was okay. I had allowed death to occur, and it was not annihilation. It was only the loss of an imaginary limit—a phony identity.

The next day, I spontaneously entered nirvikalpa samadhi again, while soaking in the bathtub. The episode lasted several minutes and was completely free of fear from the beginning. The bright pleasure simply increased until the separate "I"-sense was overwhelmed in light.

From October on, each time I sat to meditate, I entered the shining void (at times remaining in samadhi for an hour or more). It is like entering deep sleep while remaining wide awake. It is luminous clarity: dreamless awakeness—pure consciousness without content other than its own uncreated bliss.

After a couple months of this, I dreamed one dawn in January 1994 that I was on a stage before an audience. A coffin was displayed on a stand and I was lying in it, facedown and naked. An emcee was on stage, and it was clear that I was to perform a Houdini-like escape act: I was supposed to free myself and emerge from the coffin.

I began to chuckle. What was the big deal? I was already free. The coffin lid was open, and I had no chains or shackles on me in the first place. I simply stood up.

Next, I was holding beautiful blue pearls in my hand, and the emcee told me to string them together as fast as I could. I started slipping the blue pearls onto a string, as a timer with TV-game show music ticked in the background. The emcee shouted, "Hurry, get as many beads on the string as you can!" For a few seconds I rapidly strung pearls, but then I stopped and looked across at the emcee. *Why do I need to do this?* I thought. *This is your game, not mine.* I gazed at the audience and all eyes were upon me. I smiled at the people as I stepped off the stage and began handing out the blue pearls, one to each person.

Then I woke up. It was a sunny winter morning in Tallahassee, Florida. I went downstairs and sat to meditate . . . and . . .

There was nowhere to go.

I strolled outdoors into the woods around my home. I saw no dilemma at all, within or without. No thing to seek. No experience to shed. No limit. I was not a something that could travel to someplace. I could not go deeper or higher through any means.

I burst out laughing from down in my belly. *THIS IS IT.* What a punch line! I thought the moment of satori would never end. But by the afternoon, when I went to pick up my sons from elementary school, I realized that satori, too, is only a state. It comes and goes. Nothing lasts.

And guess what? I don't care in the least. I am not dismayed when ego appears, or when it disappears. I am no longer at war with ego or void. They are twin aspects of consciousness itself. I don't take sides at all.

Reality is not samadhi, the extinguishing of all forms. Reality is not even satori, the natural mode of egolessness. Reality is no special state at all; no special condition. Reality is the *IS* of all possible states, their origin and unqualified basis, perfectly open and unbounded; pure capacity. Fundamentally, nothing has changed or ever will, and what I've come to understand was already only so: Just *this*.

From a certain perspective it can seem a big deal: I've *grokked* my own essence, and it is reality (or Buddha-nature). Or, as the Persian poet, Omar Khayam, put it: "I am myself, Heaven and Hell."

But on the other hand, Buddha-nature and a buck will buy me a buck's worth of groceries. No big deal. No special status. Nothing special at all.

These days, I sometimes meditate for pleasure and refreshment, like drinking a delicious tea. And I occasionally enter spontaneous mystic states during meditation. Even so, not any of it is necessary; and none of it is greater than simple happiness. Samadhi or no samadhi, satori or no satori, ego or no ego—there is no limit, already. No dilemma.

Nothing is *more* than wonderful. This moment is wonderful. Nothing is *more* than whole. This moment is complete. THIS is as God as it gets.

Truth (or joy) is not exclusive, not hidden, not vague or abstract, not elsewhere, *not different than the stream of life*. Birth and change and death are aspects of a single process, the *only* event: the activity of (or within) Reality. Nothing exists but Bright Mystery, which forever flows as all the possibilities of life in all the worlds. As Lao Tzu put it: "The Way that can be deviated from is not the Great Way."

It is not that I am now at every moment floating along in a mood of blissful clarity, or that my neuroses have utterly evaporated. "After enlightenment," I still at times feel frustrated, angry, and so forth. I also feel saddened by the intense sufferings of our human world family. But I do not resist any of it. Whether pleasure or pain is arising, I understand the empty and inherently free nature of the stream of endless changes, and I see there is no escape, nowhere else to go. I can only be whole (without alternative), abiding as the Heart.[6]

It took twenty-two years of spiritual searching from the moment I first encountered the "clear light mind" to finally accept the wholeness that I am, the same totality that is true of everyone.

Friend, hear what I say: The Divine you seek is *your own identity*, before all ego-dilemma. Therefore, be already at ease. Relax into your own life-process. Trust in happiness, luminous and clear. Reality is Wholly Spirit, the Light that, while transcending every personality, also shines as all our life stories. In the midst of experience we are fundamentally free, beyond words and beyond worlds.

---

[6] Following the tradition of Indian sages of non-dual wisdom (*Advaita*), I often use the term "Heart" (*Hridayam*) to refer to unqualified consciousness or uncreated (inherent) intelligence.

1

Naming the Nameless

The Way that can be told is not the Great Way
The name you can say is not the real name.
Terms may be used, but none of them are absolute.

(First lines from the *Tao Teh Ching* of Lao Tzu)

Paradoxically, in order to begin talking about what is ultimately nameless, we first need a name! Calling it "The Nameless" is already assigning a name tag. I hesitate to use the name "God" because that term is so overburdened with centuries of religious and anti-religious baggage that it has become too heavy to manage. I also steer clear of other male-hierarchy names such as "Lord" and "Master." Instead, over the years, I have found the following terms to be useful in my own contemplation of truth, and these are the ones you'll mostly see throughout this book (I have chosen to capitalize these names as an act of respect):

- **Reality**—the timeless, immutable condition, untouched by the endless changes of the cosmos; yet, paradoxically, the very ground of the cosmos of total fluctuation.

- **Mystery**—the unknowable Being or Condition of all appearances, objective and subjective.

- **Heart**—an ancient term for Reality, because one intuits and <u>feels</u> the inherent Mystery of life at the center of one's being. In relation to the physical body, one senses the seat of the "I" thought in the chest region, slightly to the right side. Esoterically, this has been linked to the heart's sino-atrial node or "pacemaker."

- **Beloved**—the source of everything one truly loves, now and forever. Also, this name honors the blissfully intimate rapport between the explicate cosmos and implicate source, which rapport (inter-being, or inter-subjectivity, or inter-exchange) can truly be called "erotic."

- **Wholeness**—the absolutely inclusive condition that does not reject or negate a single atom of the total cosmos.

- **Continuum**—a physics term that refers to manifest reality: the totality of patterns within ever-greater patterns, in which space-time-matter-energy is an indivisible field, and all that appears is mutually dependent on everything else.

- **Radiant Life (the Current of Life)**—the primordial power which is the source-light of all forms of energy and matter, and which is experienced in the body-mind as a circulating current of self-luminous, living and intelligent force.

- **True (Original) Nature**—our native, inherent, uncaused essence.

- **The Great Way**—a translation of the Chinese word, *Tao*, signifying that <u>all</u> things are process, event, FLOW. Everything changes, nothing lasts. Therefore, "I" is more precisely a verb than a noun.

Notes on the Teacher

A common mistake students of spiritual paths make is to identify the teaching with the teacher, and so to think that various qualities of the teacher's personality are critical aspects of the Way.

For example, if you had gone to a meditation retreat led by my late friend, the Zen teacher Scott Morrison, who exuded a cozy and amiable personality, you might have come to believe the Way is mostly about developing a motherly warm heart and a childlike, sweet-tempered innocence—just like Scott Morrison.

Imagine your shock when you go to a meditation retreat led by a teacher who holds a high-ranking black belt in karate, and who teaches the Way in a martial manner: "Suffering is your own activity, superimposed on the openness of experience," he booms, glaring at you. "So cut the crap and quit your whining, NOW!" Students of this samurai-like teacher may well come to believe that the Way is mostly about developing courage and sharpening the sword of wisdom that severs clinging.

But no one's personality or particular style of teaching is itself the Way; these are just the media, the delivery-system, for the message. Ultimately, the message is not found in the words or even the practices given, but in the irrepressible signal that alerts your heart to its own greatness.

All authentic teachers are demonstrating the universal Way, but because each has a particular personality and background, the teachings come out "flavored" by the teacher's own character—most importantly, by the teacher's own strengths and weaknesses.

Many seekers have been fed the myth that awakened persons are "perfect." That's freaking ridiculous! It is precisely this dangerous lie that has led to a number of idolatrous personality-cults.

A genuine awakening to the freedom of essential being does not perfect any personality. Awakening runs deeper than the personality—it is to fully contact life at the Heart, prior to the emergent personality—while not excluding everything that is body and mind.

We certainly do not need to become "perfect" (whatever that god-awful word implies) in order to truly awaken. Nor does awakening radically change our personalities. Rather, enlightenment is an opening to a new, free orientation to one's personality and all the many other functions that make up a life.

Alan Watts and Chogyam Trungpa, two of the better-known spiritual teachers in the West, were both addicted to cigarettes and alcohol. Heart disease killed each of them while relatively young (and AIDS may have played a role in the death of Trungpa). Yet their lucid teachings (I recommend the books of both men) seem quite genuine and helpful. How the hell can this be? Both these guys had serious flaws.

Because enlightenment doesn't make you perfect! Awakening doesn't take away the operation of the genes, or the born personality. It also doesn't cure AIDS.

It's best to work with a teacher you naturally resonate with, someone who talks straight to your heart. But it's also good to meet a few other teachers, get a taste of their different teaching styles. Then you'll discern more clearly the seasonings your own teacher has added to the cosmic Way.

Don't be naïve. Spiritual teachers—lamas, roshis, rebbes, sheiks, gurus—are <u>people</u>: women and men who have awakened (to varying degrees) to fundamental freedom and then integrated (to varying degrees) this understanding into their personal lives. Everyone who awakens to transcendental being expresses enlightenment with unique quirks and charms, weaknesses and strengths. EVERYONE!

PART ONE

Ego Is Natural

ADYASHAKTI

Zombies Need Not Apply

Seekers like to idealize "egoless" persons. Gurus, saints and spiritual masters are supposedly "egoless". I've spent time in the company of a number of famous gurus and not one of them was egoless. A few of them, in fact, were egomaniacs (but that's a different point).

It's boorish at best to be an egomaniac. But, on the other hand, there is no use striving to be "egoless." Even the greatest Buddhas who ever lived had functioning egos. You can be certain of this, because to be without a functioning ego is to be utterly helpless.

There are only five completely egoless states:

- newborn babies
- deep (dreamless) sleep
- coma or vegetative states
- trance-absorption in formless, super-mental consciousness.[7]

---

[7] A Sanskrit term for this state is *nirvikalpa samadhi*. I prefer to call it *deep wake*, or *dreamless wake*, since it is to enter the previously "unconscious" realm of deep sleep while remaining wide awake. It is the experience of awareness prior

None of these egoless states is permanent (even coma is resolved at death). If you are not presently abiding in one of these temporary egoless states, then be assured, you are not presently egoless.

In the fullness of enlightenment the ego arises and works just fine. The "I" sense is apparent, but it does not hamper the feeling of free being. Ego—the individual-bodily-self point of view—is recognized as an operating program for organizing experience and functioning in the world.

The operating program called ego emerges from both "hardware" and "software." The "hardware" of ego pertains to the brain's wiring for language and thought; the "software" of ego refers to cultural conditionings and individual experiences overlaid on the self-idea."[8]

Ego is handy for driving a car, buying groceries, writing books on enlightenment, cashing huge royalty checks, paying taxes, etc., and it remains transparent to the mood of wonder, humor and freedom. Then, during periods of formal meditation (and also deep sleep), when awareness relaxes beyond even the noticing of external or internal data, ego melts away like a salt doll dropped into the ocean.

There is no need to kill the ego. No possibility of it, either! Just see it for what it is. In

---

to all qualifications—a luminous boundless void that Buddhists have called Original Face or Clear Light Mind.

[8] In large part, the ego-construct is based on language. Prior to about two years old, an infant is basically egoless. Then children rapidly develop the ability to talk and at the same time acquire a conceptual self-image: "I," "me," "myself," "mine." These factors together—brain-wiring, cultural overlays and personal experiences—form the ego, the self-system named "I."

periods of stillness and quiet investigation (meditation), learn to see beyond the software. To fear or hate ego is a belly-ache from partially digested Eastern philosophy. Mature teachings have criticized this futile path of trying to destroy the ego.

1. Ego-"I" is not _within_ (interior) to the body-mind. "I" names the _whole_ body-mind.

2. Ego-"I" (the whole body itself) is the sophisticated creation of billions of years of psycho-physical evolution.

3. There is nothing independent about ego. "I" is a functional unit of the total cosmos.

4. The multi-dimensional human body-mind _itself_ is ego, and it is the crown of creation!

5. Acknowledge the ordeal of Original Mind evolving in biological form: amoebas to trilobites to dinosaurs to primates to hominids to self-consciousness (ego). Praise the ego!

You can _try_ to eliminate or block the ego. (But ask yourself who is trying, pal.) Or, you can live each moment as Wholeness, in which case, you'll find that ego comes and goes all by itself. Where is ego during moments of deeply focused involvement—the "flow" of athletes, musicians and artists? Ego also vanishes in deep sleep and meditation, during passionate lovemaking, and in many other moments of "flow."

Whether ego appears or disappears, ego is not the enemy. The "I"-sense does not prevent happiness or enlightenment. Indeed, even after a person enjoys oceanic states of ego-dissolution, of absolutely selfless being, the ego-"I" comes back on-line, all by itself. This should not be surprising: after all, every night the ego vanishes in deep sleep, and every morning it pops up again in the waking state. This tells you all you need to know about the ordinary usefulness of the "I"-program.

"I" is not our True Nature, and not everlasting. Again, it is only a biologically-based system for organizing experience and bodily functioning. But as long as it appears, "I" is a feature in the process of True Nature. Like the ocean is waving, God (Who else?) is ego-ing. "I" is an aspect of Original Mind.

Not the much-maligned ego, but rather, separative *activity*—the unwillingness to love, to relate, to participate, to share, to *live as peace*—is the true obstruction of happiness.

Understood?

Now let's live and work and play and die without beating our poor heads against an imaginary problem. <u>You</u> and <u>me</u>. Zombies need not apply.

Vitamin-E Cures Gunshot Wounds to the Head

Have you noticed that we sometimes exaggerate the benefits of things that we find helpful and useful in our lives? This tendency seems especially pronounced when it comes to spiritual paths. Teachers and students and scriptural writings typically overstate the glories of enlightenment while ignoring the natural imperfections of every human personality—including "awakened beings."[9] Various groups aggrandize their own teachers and lineage ("My guru can out-teach your guru."). Some scriptures even mention *samyak sambodhi*—"perfect, unsurpassable enlightenment"—as if certain extraordinary human beings have become purified of all shadows.[10] What dangerous nonsense! Again and

---

[9] The wonderful Zen teacher, Shunryu Suzuki said, "Strictly speaking, there are no enlightened people, there is only enlightened activity." In other words, no person is in possession of enlightenment; people simply act happy and free in moments of open awareness—or not.

[10] During my early years of spiritual seeking, I spent time with teachers from the West and also from India, Korea, Tibet and Southeast Asia—and not one of them was without blind-spots, weaknesses and shadows. After all, they were human beings—like you and me! This is why Zen teachers

again, this claim has been the set-up for financial and sexual exploitation of students by "perfect masters."

I believe we inflate and embellish our spiritual paths because our idealism and hopefulness runs away with us. We project our ideals onto our teachers; we mistake archetypes (such as statues of a beatifically smiling Buddha seated in deep repose) for actual flesh-and-blood persons; we judge ourselves to be unsatisfactory and lacking, and we hope someday to become perfectly adorable. In short, we lean toward the future and the great "something" that is to come. Of course, this runs counter to simple awakening, which is to *utterly relax into the present moment as we <u>are</u>.*

Let's come down to earth for a moment and examine what enlightenment *won't* do:

- **Make you physically immortal.** It won't even make you physically *fit.* The "deathlessness" spoken of in mystical texts refers to one's original being, not to the born body. All suggestion of actual physical immortality is laugh-out-loud silliness. "Immortal masters" who have supposedly live for centuries in the Himalayas or the forests of India are no more real than leprechauns. (As for physical fitness, it is no secret that to achieve and maintain it, you must <u>eat well</u> and <u>work out</u>—aerobic and strength-training and stretching, three or more times a week—*plus* learn to relax. END OF STORY!)

---

recommend that we "Kill the Buddha," rather than turn him (or her) into a Superhero.

- **Make you a perfect human being.**
  Surprisingly enough, awakening to
  freedom—liberation from the limits of
  conventional ego-identity—won't
  necessarily even make you a nicer person. If
  it did, we wouldn't have abusive and
  exploitive gurus, at least some of whom
  actually are "advanced" adepts. That is why
  Tibetan Buddhism, to name one path,
  emphasizes again and again the need to
  develop *both* wings of enlightenment:
  <u>wisdom</u> (the unqualified consciousness of
  the Heart) and <u>compassion</u> (the motivation
  and ability to love and serve all beings).

- **Make you a genius in all of life's
  pursuits.** Too many spiritual teachers have
  grabbed up musical instruments or a
  paintbrush, imagining themselves (just
  because they are "enlightened") to be
  brilliant at *all* endeavors—only to make us
  wince at the horribly amateurish kitsch they
  call "enlightened music" or "enlightened
  art."

- **Cure cancer, etc.** Sri Ramakrishna, Ramana
  Maharshi and Lex Hixon died from cancer.
  These three men were illuminated teachers,
  remarkably awake and alive in spirit.

- **Protect you from random misfortune.**
  Thomas Merton, the brilliant Catholic
  mystic, while visiting Bangkok as the
  keynote speaker at a religious conference,
  was electrocuted by the frayed wiring of an
  electric fan when he stepped out of a
  bathtub onto wet tiles.

- **Cure neurosis.** There is a well-known Tibetan lama who suffered manic-depressive illness; an American roshi who took Prozac for depression. Meditation by itself—even the breakthrough of genuine awakening— does not usually complete the work of healing neurosis, especially the emotional problems that stem from relationships, sexual and otherwise. The body-centered psychotherapies (as opposed to "talk therapy")—Bio-Energetics, Gestalt, etc.— are often better equipped for this psycho-physical work than simple meditation. Other illnesses, such as manic-depressive disorder, are apparently caused by imbalanced brain metabolism and respond best to medications.

- **Cure addictions.** Nisargadatta Maharaj chain-smoked until he died of heart disease. Alan Watts, a chain-smoking alcoholic, also died from heart disease. Yet another chain-smoking alcoholic, Chogyam Trunpga, died from AIDS. Yet all three of these addicted men were gifted teachers, who in many ways seemed awake.

- **AND HERE IS THE ONLY THING ENLIGHTENMENT *WILL* DO:** Awaken you to the freedom and clarity that are the nature of ordinary awareness, now and *now-ever.*

Ego Is Entirely Okay

A common misunderstanding among those engaged in a spiritual practice is that there is something wrong or even diabolical about ego ("I," "me," "my, "mine"). In fact, these cognitions are natural functions of the body-mind and language and need not be (nor *can* they be) eradicated. Ego comes and goes all by itself. (Where is ego during dreamless sleep?)

Ego is not an entity, but an *activity*—not (properly) a noun, but a verb. Ego-"I" does not, in itself, *live*. Ego-"I" is <u>lived</u> in and of the Great and Total Process of Reality. In other words, the phenomenal "I" is not the Self—not a living identity. There is Only God, the Continuum, and such Real Identity is infinite and unknowable.

Ego-"I" is given; not self-existent, but *produced*, emerging and disappearing spontaneously. "I" is not solid, not ultimate or fundamental. Ego-"I" is only a program, a composite pattern within Reality. The Real Self gives rise to the self-image (ego-"I") through language and memory.

There is no need to establish, protect, preserve, improve or even monitor ego. There is no need to hate, fear or destroy ego-"I." Reality is not in the least concerned about ego-"I." Ego (the functional mind) in itself is already not a hindrance, not the root-cause of suffering.

But the root-cause of suffering is *misidentification* with this constructed "I." This case of mistaken identity leads to <u>attachment</u> (both clinging and avoiding), which causes suffering. Again: The <u>root</u>-cause of suffering is not the simple psycho-physical arising of ego-"I" (which is a functional event, not a problem) but the *misidentification* with ego-"I".

Such misidentification arises from mistaking memory (which merely symbolizes real experience) to *be* real experience. The tools of thought and language and imagination then concretize (reify) the ego-"I". You believe that you remember your "self" as a continuous entity lasting over the years, when, in truth, ego-"I" is only the activity of this moment.

Therefore, liberation from suffering is necessarily liberation from false identification with ego-"I", and *thus* the relaxation of attachment to things and events. In other words, liberation is moving out of false identification with limitation into the free intuition of infinity.

Real experience is now. It can't be recorded in memory. (That which is recorded in memory is only a *symbol* of real experience.)

Real identity is now. It can't be captured or reduced in any way. (Whatever is captured and reduced is not real, but abstract—a mere symbol.)

Real Experience is *exactly the same* as Real Identity. The Platonic metaphysics that disdains the body and all sensory experience as illusion has been misguiding seekers for centuries. The continuum of all things appearing and changing and disappearing is without dilemma. Unobstructed present experience is already the enjoyment of freedom and luminosity.

Ego-"I" keeps on emerging and submerging without being a hindrance to Identity, because "I" is transparent to awareness. It is simply obvious that ego is only an objectified or projected self—a concept, a software program for organizing experience.

Re-cognize "I" for what it is, and the Heart will enjoy freedom at infinity, even as the body-mind and total world continue to flow.

Enlightenment Is Enlightened Activity

Enlightenment is the intuition of the transcendence of the usual limits of thought and identity—a going beyond the confined self, stuck inside a bag of flesh in the box of the space-time material universe. It is awakening to a timeless, limitless awareness that is infinitely expanded and free.

Yet enlightenment cannot be described as some particular state or experience. Rather, it is the *way* of present openness to whatever arises, within and without. Enlightenment is enlightened activity: It is to look and act and feel free and whole NOW.

Any <u>experience</u> of enlightenment (epitomized by moments of breakthrough, called in Zen, *satori*, or *kensho*) is temporary. Nobody goes around in a permanent state of satori. THERE ARE NO PERMANENT STATES OF ANY KIND. Nothing lasts. Indeed, this is one of the key realizations that lead to the *attitude* of enlightenment, an attitude of freedom and humor and equanimity. And one must add: iconoclasm. Enlightened people tend to convey a wild sense of humor—an attitude of laughing at structures of every kind.

The enlightened attitude develops over time, following naturally upon the experience of awakening. From that *attitude* (or *orientation*—more ongoing than any experience, no matter how profound) the *enlightened way of life* emerges. If enough people were awake to this attitude, there could even be an *enlightened culture*! (Or at least, an enlightened group of friends!)

The Living World Is Not Concerned

Real Life is not at all concerned about trying to make ego-"I" disappear, or about returning to Source. This is because:

1. Ego-"I" is already no hindrance to open, luminous being.
2. Life (or the totality of functioning) is *never*—not for an instant—separate from its own source.

Try on a new way of viewing life:

- The free, radiant nature of the total living being *already* transcends ego: it gives rise to ego as its own spontaneous play in the many worlds of cosmos.
- Source is never at war with its own manifestation.
- The purpose of life is *not* return to its Source. <u>The purpose of life is simply Reality.</u> (Life *IS* the Source <u>Alive</u>—in spontaneously flowing manifestation.)

Forget Trying to Deny the Body

"Apart from the body does the world exist? Has anyone seen the world without the body?" Ramana Maharshi

Who can deny the born bodily being? The incarnational process, the play of individuality? The individual is not ultimate, not permanent; but neither does a song last forever, yet that fact does not make music less appealing.

I, the apparent individual, won't last forever. However, the source of each temporary individual *is* everlasting. There is no God, no Self, nor Reality that renounces the ego. Indeed, Reality Itself is ego-ing. Reality is constantly being born *as* apparent individuals.

There is no such thing as ultimate independence. The Wholeness of Existence cannot be reduced to a radically separate unit, a part that is intrinsically isolatable or permanent or self-existing.

Yet there is certainly *relative* or *functional* independence. For example, if we both have to urinate, and you use the restroom first, I still have to urinate! This functional level of individuality cannot be negated. Every "I" is a temporary (mortal) wave of a timeless (immortal) Ocean.

The body is a process. The whole process cannot be reduced to an inner self or ego. The whole body *itself* is the ego (or "I"-process).

The body (ego) cannot be negated, but only transcended.

To wit, these words from the modern Indian sage, Ramana Maharshi:

> To those who have not realized the Self as well as to those who have, the word 'I' refers to the body, but with this difference: that for those who have not realized the Self, the 'I' is confined to the body, whereas for those who have realized, the 'I' shines as the limitless Self.

> To those who have not realized the Self as well as to those who have, the world is real. But to those who have not realized, Truth is adapted to the measure of the world, whereas to those who have realized, Truth shines as the Formless Perfection, the Substratum of the world. This is all the difference between them.

Beware Nihilism

"It is better not to begin. Having begun, it is better
to go all the way." (Zen saying)

Don't set about dying unless you're willing to go all
the way to become reborn. The Hero's Journey is
not meant to be a one-way trip. After your spiritual
adventures, you come back home with your boon for
your friends. Consider the ancient Buddhist chant
from the Heart Sutra: "Gone, gone, gone beyond,
gone beyond going beyond; fully awake, so be it."
Notice what follows "going beyond"—"going *beyond*
going beyond."

One-way trips can put you dangerously out
of balance. Deconstructing your life and mind down
to zero, seeing that all your meanings and
conditionings are ultimately void, continuing in this
path but stopping short of liberation is <u>not</u>
recommended! Where you encounter intellectuals
who have stopped short—at nihilism,
meaninglessness, nothingness—you meet some
profoundly unhappy characters.

Beware ego-death without rebirth and re-
integration. Beware nihilism. You must continue all
the way through the process to rebirth and new life.

Reality is not opposed to ego-"I". It
includes ego-"I". The body-mind personality is not

(inherently) problematic, and does not (inherently) need fixing.

"I" is a convention of language and thought; it begins to develop at about two years old (not coincidentally) with the acquisition of speech. "I" is hard-wired, like speech, and develops on its own. "I" is natural and inevitable. "I" (in and of itself) is not a problem, <u>not</u> the cause of suffering. Anyone lacking this self-organizing feature of mind, ego-"I", would be about as functional as a head of cabbage.

On the other hand, mistaking this organizing faculty of intelligence, "I", as your very <u>identity</u> IS the central cause of suffering! The chief symptom of this suffering is fear, the sense of separated, encapsulated, limited, threatened existence. The conventional attempts to cure this fear can be seen in endless secular and religious strategies throughout history. NONE OF THEM WORK.

The only effective "cure" for such fear is the awakening of the heart-mind beyond its bondage to the false identification with ego-"I". Then consciousness is released to trust and love and laugh, to feel the Unqualified Openness of freedom from limitation.

Language, imaging, abstraction, knowledge, experience, meaning—all must be deconstructed (death) and allowed to reappear within the new perspective of wholeness (rebirth). Everyone must die and be reborn. That very theme is one of the oldest and most universal ways of summarizing the spiritual path. But, ego-"I" does not need to be destroyed, or healed, or saved, or changed—only <u>understood</u> for what it is: a natural program evolved through billions of years of life and adaptation to become an excellent conscious agent of Infinity.

Why destroy "I"? Do you want to regress to life as a trilobite? It took billions of years of universal and planetary evolution to build "I". And now you're eager to eradicate it? Get real. God, or Reality, is *being* "I". Isn't that obvious?

Why not live as the "I" of Life? Be the "I" of Love (as in, "I love you."). It's easier than suffering, more fun and takes less energy.

The Seeker's Dilemma

Have you tried getting rid
Of what you haven't got?
It always will elude you.

You can chant and pray,
Meditate all day,
Try Scuba Yoga ™ —"It's NEW!"

You can fast till you faint,
Live like a saint
Or break every religious taboo

You can memorize the Gita
And eat vegan pita
Build a self-composting loo

You can stand on your head
Till your nose has bled
Earn a black belt in Kung Fu

You can huff and puff
Till your body is buff,
And screw your Tantric guru

But getting rid
Of what already is not
Is impossible to do.

Nothing Special

I am not special. From start to finish, within and without, low and high, there is not anything about me that is radically different than any human being who has ever lived or will live.

I am not special, but I am awake. Like Gautama, I am not a "Buddhist"; like Gautama, I am a Buddha. I am the Heart. I recognize that I am always, already awake.

Therefore, I do not practice a spiritual path that leads gradually or suddenly to enlightenment. I practice only awakeness; I practice what I *am*. My spiritual discipline is simply to abide as I am (not *less* than I am) in the present moment, and thus to forever actualize the Heart in all dimensions of an integrated life.

PART TWO

Awareness Itself Is the Way

ADYASHAKTI

Get with the Program

"The Force That Must Be Forced Is Not the True Force."
Lao Tzu

It is counter-productive to be busily straining to "surrender harder." You cannot huff and puff and bring about the cessation of your own ego.

Rather, the natural process of conscious awakening progresses in the surrendered mood of trust that Christian mystics call "waiting on the Lord" or "Remembrance," and Buddhists call "mindfulness." That disposition is most true and helpful. The Christian phrase "waiting on the Lord" does not mean waiting on the Lord to arrive (from beyond the asteroid belt); God (Reality, Identity) is always, already fully present now. It means resting heart-breath-attention in the Presence, without self-concern. In other words, if you were to offer a prayer while truly "waiting on the Lord," the feeling-intelligence of your entire prayer would be, *Amen* ("So BE it.") Not incidentally, "Amen" makes an effective mantra of peace.

Or you could just say "Yes."

"Yes" is the Word. Like "Amen," "Yes" is a complete prayer. The powerful grace of gratitude, acceptance, no-resistance, openness and flow is in the heartfelt attitude of "Yes."

Total acceptance is total release.
Amen.

Wholeness Is Not Private

Already, there is no separate entity, no exclusive identity. Just as there is no independent self who dies, there is no independent self who becomes free.

No separate, isolated self ever attains enlightenment. The only one who could be enlightened is *already* wholeness, totality, absolute singularity. Enlightenment is simply reality, already. All-inclusive: mosquitoes and rainbows intermingled.

Put into Judeo-Christian-Islamic theological language: No special action is needed to worship the Divine. Already, there is no *other* than the Beloved, God of all life, "low" and "high." Already, there is nothing but worship in truth. All the worlds are only sacrifice in God. Grace is our free condition. Therefore we may freely and gladly relax into life, without exaggeration. The simplest and also the most profound way to Love God and Thank God and Live God, is to smile as the whole body and breathe easily—releasing everything and accepting the fullness, while taking care of what is now at hand.

As for non-theological language: No special attainment is necessary to enjoy reality, our essential nature. Reality is uncreated. It is our free condition, and does not require maintenance. Reality cannot be grasped or controlled, but only understood and lived.

In my own case, when I awoke to the real situation, nothing happened. Nothing changed. Enlightenment makes no difference. Everything is just what it is; except that I am happy, no longer seeking happiness.

***

Enlightenment is like this: When I was 18, I climbed to the top of Mt. Audubon in the Rockies. When I reached the peak I found a small, metal notebook tucked under the edge of a boulder: the mountain's guestbook, with pages on which to sign one's name.

But there was no pencil!

I sat there, amused that I had climbed so high but was unable to register my achievement. Then I felt something crawling up my calf. Ants. At the pinnacle of the second tallest mountain in the American Rockies, tiny red ants made their home.

In closing, I offer this poem:

Stand on lofty mountain,
Nowhere to leave a name.
Freedom is not private.
With us always, all sentient beings.

Light and Enlightenment

- The term "awake" (in Sanskrit, *bodhi*) refers to transcendent wisdom, and is synonymous with the term "enlightenment." The term enlightenment, however, can be misleading, since the word literally means "condition of inner light." It implies that experiences of inner light are the same as awakening to one's inherent nature.

- Experiences of inner light are phenomena of the subtle body[11]; they come and go like all other phenomena. But awakening to the real condition does not occur within the limits of any realm in the great stream of changes.

- True awakening is not of the nature of a vision, a thought, a sensation, or a new and extraordinary experience. It is not anything that is *added* to the body-mind. True awakening is the gradual or sudden

---

[11] This higher conscious dimension of the whole body-mind goes by various names. In Western mysticism, it is called the astral body or energy body; in Buddhism, it is known as *sambhogakaya* (literally: the body of highest emotion— usually translated as "Body of Delight").

understanding and abiding <u>as</u> unqualified consciousness—the Heart—which already is Reality. It is a breakthrough to what you already *are*, before the beginning and after the end of time.

- The process of awakening to the Heart may be attended by a tremendous release of energy. This unleashed energy (called *kundalini* in many Eastern mystical traditions, and *Holy Spirit* or *Fire of God* in Western schools) is felt as a powerful current coursing up and down the spinal circuit and flowing through various other subtle channels in the body and brain and even above and beyond the physical body, to a Godhead of Light infinitely above. The kundalini can produce dramatic experiences of inner light and other effects in the body-mind. But it must be understood that these experiences are signs of the activation of latent life-force; blissful, yes, but not <u>in themselves</u> transcendent awareness. In other words, these experiences (while intensely pleasurable) do not <u>produce</u> awakening, so much as <u>accompany</u> it.

- Psychedelic drugs can produce experiences of light in the brain and elsewhere in the subtle energy body. Certain yogic postures and breathing exercises can also stimulate the nervous system to cause a release of energy and an experience of inner light. Epileptics, as well, observe a variety of lights within. But, obviously, not every drug user or yogi or epileptic is enlightened!

- Just so, not every person who experiences wonderful inner lights—not even the "thousand-petal lotus of light" at the crown and above—has necessarily <u>understood</u> the nature of these and all other phenomena, physical or subtle. Only when the Heart of <u>all</u> experience—"low" or "high"—is radically intuited, has real awakening dawned.[12]

- What is true awakening? It is not another incident of *becoming*—not a change in state—but the *direct gnosis*, beyond all states, of original freedom. It is to radically intuit, presume and <u>be</u> the free Heart of everything that appears and disappears. It is to abide as unqualified consciousness, which is reality delighting in reality.

---

[12] Having said all this, it is a fact that (in meditation, at least) nearly every awakened woman or man <u>feels</u> and <u>sees</u> and <u>hears</u> the Light, or radiance of the Heart, both within and without the body-mind. This is because our multi-dimensional life is a play upon indestructible Light, and when the mind becomes very still and deep, the vibratory radiance is spontaneously revealed.

The Great Perfection

Reality does not need to be attained. Reality does not need to be maintained. Reality does not require seeking from the point of view of separation and limitation. Reality does not demand self-concerned efforts within duality.

Reality does not yield to explanations (maps, models and analytical constructs; analogies and metaphors). There is no final "figuring it all out" or "getting it right." Reality is utterly prior to and beyond all thoughts, words and images. Reality is prior to and beyond all experience, knowledge and imagination. Reality is perfectly free of all information (form) and all meaning (formal relationships). Yet it includes all of these, and excludes nothing whatsoever.

Reality—the Transcendental Living Intelligence—is not a special prize that can be won or lost. Likewise, the dream-adventure of bodily life is not some terrible game that must be won or lost.

There is only Reality, already. Already and always there exists no independence at all (and thus, no independent entity). There is simply no such one. "I" (the sense of an independent or separate self) comes and goes as a mental formation. It is a fleeting permutation within the absolute singularity of totality. But Reality has no arriving and departing. It is only immutably whole.

All seeking is motivated by dilemma, the sense of separation from Whole Life. But ironically, all seeking is an exercise (or dramatization) of that very dilemma—an acting out of the idea that Reality (God, the Beloved) is yet to be, and must be reached through a process of becoming. Enlightenment, however, is not a matter of becoming (self-improvement, changes of state); enlightenment is a matter of *being*. Seeking the Beloved becomes, at last, impossible. The separative predicament of the seeker is recognized as un-Real, and the orientation toward self-effort is obviated.

This freedom of "No dilemma!"—release from problem-based seeking—does not communicate itself through argument, debate, logic or information—that is, by convincing the rational, discursive mind of its truth. The freedom of "No dilemma!" communicates directly in heart-felt intuition of Reality, prior to the rational, discursive mind. "No dilemma!" suddenly stands out as the Obvious, the Real, the tacitly understood, prior to any movement toward knowing (grasping).

THEREFORE, LEAVE GOD ALONE.

Relax all seeking, all self-motivated striving, all strategies of self-improvement, all controlling. Come to *rest* in God (in the Heart, *as* the Heart). *Be as you are*, and let everything that appears come and go in its own way. Be awake to the truth that all that appears is only a variation of the God-Light. Everything happening is already sacrificial worship of God. Even such ungodly events as terrorist attacks display the truth of impermanence and the tragic consequences of the ignorance of Love.

The sounds of the birds and the garbage truck are mantra. The experiences of making love and paying the bills are mudra. Every appearance is in and of God; everything is a temporary modulation of the Pure Signal of Existence-Consciousness-Bliss. God, the Irreducible Mystery, is paradoxically That Which Is Always Known (through all that appears). Just so, God is beyond all names, yet every name necessarily refers to God. This ultimate realization is called, in Tibetan Buddhism, *Maha Ati*, the Great Perfection, or *Mahamudra*, the Great Sign. It is the completion stage of awakening.

Dear sister or brother, hear this truth: The divine demand is not that you continuously seek God in your scary, private dream. The divine demand is that you release yourself into your Divine Condition. You must *live* God, now. If *you* are not being Buddha, your world is bereft of Buddhas; when you *live* as Buddha, your world is populated only with Buddhas.

Reality IS

Reality is always, already the Condition, whether you are groaning from a severe toothache or moaning from a tremendous orgasm. No matter the pain or pleasure or any other kind of experience, Reality must necessarily BE the Condition. Otherwise, what kind of Reality are we talking about? One that comes and goes? Or a reality that is distant and must be reached? Or a reality that under certain circumstances is obstructed or denied? Such describes space and time and space-time limits; that does not describe Reality.

The Real Condition is always, already the case. It cannot be obtained because it is never absent. It is closer than the beat in your heart, the breath in your lungs. It is the free and unqualified Nature of the body, mind and world at *all* times— and truly beyond time.

Baptism by Spirit

The Source is not many. The Source is not one. The Source is <u>only</u>.

All the many and even the one are a self-manifesting play upon this Source alone.

The Source is not high or low, within or without. The Source is <u>only</u>.

All that is above or below, inside or outside, is a spontaneous permutation of the Source.

Therefore, the Source cannot be located or attained, or ever lost.

To seek the Source by turning upward or downward, within or without, is actually to turn away from its present *totality*.

Seeking the Source is an exercise in separation and duality, for seeking necessarily involves and maintains the independent seeker. To seek the Source is to dramatize fear, dilemma and exile. It is to presume and act out the "absence" of the Source. But the Source is not ever reached, because it is always, already infinitely <u>Here</u>.

Seekers lean toward the future in hope and dread. But tomorrow never comes, while the Source is always timelessly present.

Seekers recall the past and identify with its moments, pleasurable and painful. But those moments are gone, while the Source is forever now.

Awakening to the Source does not require further seeking. It requires the utter sacrifice of the seeker's false identification with separateness in <u>this</u> moment. Awakening to the Source demands the release of whatever you are withholding.

<u>You</u> are the necessary sacrifice.

Every mystical tradition, across all times, places and cultures, has taught that this "death" (or utter surrender) of the limited, independent identity is the sole entrance fee to the freedom and wholeness of the Source. Intuitively, every honest seeker comes to understand what is required. But not all are ready to pay the admission price.

Oh, human heart, do you <u>really</u> want the Infinite Heart?

Then abandon seeking altogether. Renounce the principle of all your concerns and self-centered labors. Admit the Whole, Unknowable Condition, Now—absolutely.

The Source will overtake you, bodily, at the instant of your true availability.

Oh, sincere seeker, your seeking will at last become too painful to continue. Your separate self will come undone and you will fall into the Source and simply <u>be</u> the Source. In that revolutionary advent, Radiant Life will awaken you whole bodily by spiritual initiation.

Such initiation is grace. Whether it is called Baptism by the Holy Spirit, by the Goddess Energy, by the Fire of God, the arousal of *Kundalini*, or any other name, it is the Eternal Life-Power that has blessed and quickened every woman and man on Earth who has ever fully awakened.

Praise the Radiant Life-Current and the graceful awakening that unclenches the navel, unknots the heart, loosens the throat, unwrinkles the forehead, relaxes the mind, opens the Eye and

*

returns attention to its birthplace and eternal home in the Source.

Enlightenment Is a Total Flop

Buddha is not a name but a title. It comes from the Sanskrit root *budh*, which means "awake." The epithet is applied to a woman or man who is awake to her own real nature. According to tradition, twenty-five-hundred years ago a group of forest monks were very impressed with the teachings of their former companion, Siddhartha Gautama, and asked him, "Are you a man or a god?" Gautama replied, "I am Awake." Thus, Siddhartha became known as Buddha (the Awake One).

There are many Buddhas throughout the East (India, Tibet, China, Japan, Korea and Southeast Asia) and also genuine Buddhas in the West. They are women and men who have awakened to the true nature of themselves and the universe.

Enlightenment confers no *uniqueness*. Enlightenment does not make you different from those who have not yet awakened. Yet some spiritual teachers expect you to literally *worship* them as the living divine! But who *isn't* the living divine?

Only Reality, the Source of everyone and everything, is the Conscious Being who is enlightened, never some separate self or independent entity. In fact, there is no such thing as *a* being; there is only Being Itself, and it is already Buddha.

You are not "other" than all that is happening now. Joy and suffering, low and high, within and without—you cannot (ultimately, perfectly) prevent or escape or control any of it. There is no alternative to totality; it is irreducible. You can only be what you already are: whole, alone, free. *Therefore, simply relax into completeness.* That's all there is to it. It is reality. It is effortless. Enlightenment is a total flop.

This reminds me of a couple Zen stories. In the first, a teacher asks a serene monk, "Are you just sitting there doing nothing?" The monk replies, "I'm not even doing that."

Here's another illustrative Zen tale:

> A Zen adept came across his student entranced in meditation. The adept asked his student what he was doing.
>
> "I'm meditating in order to become a Buddha," the student said, and returned to the depths of his absorption.
>
> The Zen adept sat nearby and began scrubbing one rock against another. The loud scraping distracted the student, who redoubled his efforts at focusing his attention on his breathing. But after a few more minutes, with his concentration broken, the student turned to the teacher and demanded to know what he was up to.
>
> "I'm polishing this rock," the teacher explained, "in order to turn it into a mirror."

The student laughed. "You can polish that rock forever," he said, "but you'll never turn it into a mirror."

"Likewise, you can meditate forever," the teacher said, "but you'll never become a Buddha."

In other words: You can never <u>become</u> free. You can only <u>be</u> free—by understanding that you are <u>already</u> free!

Speaking practically, because we may grow to understand our free nature more and more completely over time, and gradually stabilize in this liberated view, it can seem that we *become* free. However, speaking from the radical view of freedom itself, what we grow to understand is the <u>prior</u> condition of this and any moment. It is timeless awareness. It is always, already Truth.

Therefore, the so-called "sudden enlightenment" schools (Soto Zen and Dzogchen and Advaita Vedanta are prime examples) point to this immediacy of direct seeing, before and beyond time: "Wake up in *this* moment, and swallow the Pacific Ocean in one gulp!" On the other hand, sudden enlightenment is most often like the "overnight success" that comes to a hardworking painter who has developed her talent and craft for decades, when one day, unexpectedly, the true essence of her expression blossoms.

A Quote from the Upanishads

All creatures born of eggs, of wombs, of moisture
in the earth; all creatures that swim, fly or walk and
those that do not move; all these have
Consciousness as the giver of their reality, all these
are impelled by Consciousness. The Universe has
Consciousness as its Eye and as its end.

The Best Things in Life Aren't Things

The "if only" meme is everywhere common: "I could be happy, *if only* I had—"

- Great wealth.
- Great power.
- Great physical beauty.
- Great fame for my talent or skill.
- The adoration of one or more special persons in my life (romantic love).
- A certain mansion, sports car, speedboat, Lear Jet, spaceship, empire, etc.

Yet, really, you don't need any of the above to be happy. The real necessities for happiness are as follows:

- You MUST like and accept yourself.
- You MUST see beyond yourself. (See the big picture; understand that the Cosmos is not about the little *you*, so you need not take its fluctuations personally.)
- You MUST love women and you MUST love men (and bring the feminine and

masculine in your own body-mind into balance.)

- You MUST love and befriend and be intimate with the natural world.
- You MUST be comfortable with change and even chaos—the lack of absolute control.
- You MUST be comfortable with uncertainty and ignorance—the lack of absolute knowledge.
- You MUST be comfortable with paradox. (The polarities NEVER resolve into one pole or the other!)
- You MUST be reconciled with death—your own death and the death of your loved ones.
- You MUST have a sense of humor.
- You MUST have a sense of purpose—your own calling and also an intuition of the great purpose at the Heart of the whole cosmic show. (Hint: it's all about awakening to radiant openness.)

For the purposes of happiness, all the rest is optional. Even physical health, while a great blessing and advantage, is ultimately not *required* in order to be happy—which is to be released in feeling to infinity.

The Presence Cannot Be Re-Presented

Memory is not Reality, but only a symbol of actual, living experience. THIS unlimited present moment is the Reality-event and cannot be shrunk to mere information and stored as memory. THIS actual living flow cannot be summarized or told (reduced to verbal symbols). The Presence cannot be re-presented. Awaken to the freedom of THIS.

The Presence is Reality. It does not exist in any form or process or mode other than <u>wholeness</u>. Reality is *only* complete. Reality *alone* is. It is unavoidable; without alternative.

Human beings try to bring order to their experiences and to understand and integrate them by putting their experiences into words. However, words are <u>not</u> Reality; and experience organized into words, no matter how tidily constructed, is <u>not</u> Reality. Words can never be made into the Wholeness of Infinite Presence (Reality), and Reality can never be reduced to the fragmentation and limitation of words.

Knowledge is not absolute. The absolute is not known.

The absolute process—the total living cosmos—is not a knower. Life is completely and absolutely and exactly *being* itself and *enjoying* itself—but not knowing itself as a limited object (because Life Itself is not a thing, not any kind of limit). Reality must necessarily be unknowable, because all knowledge is limited, the perceiving or conceiving of an <u>object</u> (however subtle).

The truth, our perfectly undeniable (and unresolvable) condition, is Mystery. Truth is the eternal unknowability of anything and everything; it is the awe and amazement and wonder and wholeness of undefined Being Itself.

There is no independent position (no absolute point of view) from which to know what anything and everything *IS*. Points of view are not absolute. The absolute is not a point of view.

Every "solid" thing and every flowing pattern of things is only a moment, passing in Radiant Mystery. Whatever appears is merely <u>appearance</u>, structured on the body-mind (the perceiving instrument and process). All that appears is process; all is flow. No thing (and no arrangement of things) lasts. Yet all appearances are permutations of the fundamentally unlimited Bright Mystery. Mystery is necessarily the Present One, always, already (<u>beyond</u> time).

There is no separated "I," no independent entity, who exists ultimately. The isolated "I" is a thought-construct that merely appears and disappears. What exists, what moves the worlds, the Giver of Life, is not "I," but generates, sustains and transforms "I."

Reality is "I"-ing. "I" is an avatar of Reality. "I" is the temporary bodily presence and process of timeless Transcendental Life.

No God or Goddess or Divine Person or Being or Self or Power is ever found apart and "other." The personal deity is non-ultimate; not false, but not absolute.

The universe is responsive. It is a participatory universe. We co-create our experiences in unqualified relationship to universe. That truth—responsiveness, relationship, continuum—is the truth out of which is constructed the myth of the personal god. But no objective deity or divine force is ever met, encountered, observed or experienced apart from the body-mind ("I"). God or Reality is not locatable, not experienced "over and against" the field of all arising.

"I" might find "God"—but that can only occur within the realm of subject/object experience. In deepest surrender, when "I" disappears—so does "God."

Real God is not many, not two, and not even one—but ONLY. Therefore, "God" or "Goddess"—the Very Source, the Heart—is never found, but only lived.

Reality Is Not What You Think

The way is Awakening <u>from</u> subjectivity and inwardness, and <u>to</u> wholeness and radiance.

The being is only present and free. Experience is patterns arising within whole being. The stuff of the mind—thoughts, emotions—is only arising, persisting for a while and passing away. It does not *identify* the being. Reality is not *identical* to subjectivity.

Consider this: Digestion is only a <u>function</u> of Life; digestion is not an IDENTITY, not a person, not the whole being, not Life Itself. Likewise, subjectivity (mind-stuff appearing and disappearing) is only a <u>function</u> of Life; it is not an IDENTITY, not a person, not the whole being, not Life Itself.

Do not mistake mere subjectivity as reality, as identity, as defining what IS. Life is <u>infinitely</u> greater than the thoughts and emotions that endlessly come and go.

It is possible (and <u>necessary</u>) to sacrifice your attachment to subjectivity—all your imaginings and memories and reveries and moods—in open-minded relaxation into the present Source of all the starry worlds of the cosmos.

PART THREE

Buddha's Greatest Hits

ADYASHAKTI

Four Basic Facts

According to tradition, after Siddhartha Gautama (the historical Buddha) awoke to his true nature (at age 30, following eleven years of contemplative practice) he gave his first public teaching to a small group of forest monks in a deer park in Benares, in northern India. The Buddha often pointed out that he taught only two things: suffering, and its cessation. His first public discourse, on those very themes, has come to be called "The Four Noble Truths."

Although the wisdom in this book is not the exclusive property of any tradition, readers who are familiar with Buddhist teachings will recognize a similar communication. Particularly, the teachings in this book resonate with Zen Buddhism and with Dzogchen ("The Great Natural Perfection" teachings of Tibetan Buddhism). It seems fitting, then, to include Buddha's "Four Noble Truths," which form the backbone of all Buddhist paths.

Here is a free rendering of those four principles (which I call the Four Basic Facts):

First Basic Fact: (Suffering.) Conditional existence cannot grant unconditional fulfillment. Life's unending changes are frustrating, stressful and unsatisfactory to the motives of a limited, independent "self." We want what we don't have, or we have what we don't want; or even when we get what we want, we tend to suffer because the desired object or situation <u>does not last</u>. Therefore, all the possible conditions and events of any life do not (in themselves) grant freedom, happiness and completeness.

Second Basic Fact: (The causes of suffering.) Unhappiness is rooted in the erroneous presumption and dramatization of separate selfhood. Attachment (<u>clinging</u> to some things and experiences and <u>recoiling</u> from others) follows as a *symptom* of this root-error. Clinging brings stress and pain because no thing or experience lasts (everything changes). Recoiling is painful and futile because there is no real possibility of escaping the ups and downs of life.

Third Basic Fact: (Liberation from suffering.) Real freedom, happiness and completeness exist <u>intrinsically</u> and can be realized and lived. Such actualization involves a process of awakening from the false presumption of limited, independent identity, [13] and thereby, from the self-hold, the clinging and recoiling that cause suffering.[14]

Fourth Basic Fact: (A process that leads to from suffering to liberation.) The Eightfold Path of awakening from the dream of false identity:

1. **View** (appropriate vision) Consider the wisdom-teachings of the heart until they have made their home in you.

2. **Intention** (appropriate resolve): Make the heart-commitment to be awake in *this* moment.[15] Choose happiness. Your happiness is your most basic form of service to others.

3. **Honesty** (appropriate speech): Tell the truth. Communicate from the heart.

---

[13] It cannot be overemphasized that the ego-"I" construct is natural, and *ego is not a wrongfulness or problem* once understood for what it is. But prior to awakened insight, this "self-system" for organizing experience tends to shatter the wholeness of life through a conceptual sense of isolated identity. Fortunately, the illusion of separate identity can be penetrated and the heart can awaken from its trance of encapsulated, limited selfhood. Then there is release from contraction and inwardness, and into relationship, wholeness and love. Such transcendence does not involve "killing" the ego-program, but rather, seeing through and beyond it in a radically new way.

[14] Achaan Chaa, a Buddhist teacher in Thailand, puts it thus: "Let go a little and feel a little happy; let go a lot and feel a lot happy; let go completely and feel completely happy."

[15] In Buddhism, this is called, "Take the one seat."

4. **Loving-kindness** (appropriate conduct): "May all beings be happy and well." "Treat all others as you would like to be treated."

5. **Work** (appropriate livelihood): Serve the body, mind, soul, spirit, family, community and culture, and benefit the planet.

6. **Friends**[16] (appropriate association): We are all of us brothers and sisters with various strengths and weaknesses. We need each other. No one can be completely free until everyone is free.

7. **Mindfulness** (appropriate awareness): Drop opinions, hopes and fears, and see everything as it simply *is*. [17] Awareness itself is healing. Awareness is the way.

8. **Meditation** (appropriate contemplation): Practice feeling and breathing and relaxing into wholeness and the energy-river of life.

---

[16] Traditionally, this sixth aspect of the Eightfold Path is "Effort." But I believe that one's Intention (or resolve—aspect #2) will naturally result in appropriate levels of effort. In my opinion, it is better advice here to emphasize the importance of *sangha*—keeping the healthy company of supportive friends.

[17] Jiddu Krishnamurti, the Indian philosopher, called such naked, open, non-judgmental attention, "choiceless awareness." This calls to mind a Zen tale in which a man asks a teacher to give him the truth of Zen in a nutshell. The teacher writes the word, "Attention." The man says, "Come on, give me more than that." The teacher writes, "Attention, attention." The man shouts, "I asked you for the pith!" The teacher writes, "Attention, attention, attention."

The Buddhist Precepts

In many parts of the world people regularly suffer hardships of biblical proportions: war, famine, flood, pestilence. By contrast, in the developed nations of the West most of us have it relatively easy. Misfortunes beyond our control (a child with birth defects, a parent with Alzheimer's) still occur, of course, yet many of the troubles we "first-worlders" suffer are of our own making, the negative consequences of our own behavior.

The remedy for such aggravation is to exercise basic self-discipline. To this end, every spiritual path provides its own guidelines. I like the Buddhist Precepts for their simplicity. They offer a concise checklist for practicing ordinary self-control. Observing such principles does not make us immune to tragedy, but can save us from a great deal of unnecessary (self-induced) troubles and pain. Here are the five traditional precepts:

- Don't kill or hurt sentient beings (or their habitats).
- Don't take what isn't yours.
- Don't cause harm through sexual misconduct.
- Don't tell lies, and don't say hurtful and unhelpful things.

- Don't misuse intoxicants that make you careless or stupid.

I prefer to restate these traditional "don'ts" in the form of positive prescriptions:[18]

- Love and protect sentient beings (and their habitats).
- Be generous and sharing.
- Be caring and responsible in all sexual conduct.
- Tell the truth, and be careful to say kind and helpful things.
- Use intoxicants responsibly, for the purpose of celebration, not drunkenness.

In summary, the Buddhist Precepts advise us to behave at all times with love, respect, care and compassion for ourselves and others.

---

[18] Just as Christianity converts the classical Jewish precept: "Do not treat others in ways you do not wish to be treated" into a positive command: "Treat others the way you wish to be treated."

Awakened Intention

(A free-rendering of the Bodhisattva Vows of Mahayana Buddhism)

Bodhisattva literally means "Awakened Being." It is a concept from *Mahayana* (Universal Vehicle) Buddhism—from which Ch'an and Zen are derived. Whereas earlier forms of Buddhism emphasized waking up and liberating oneself, the Universal Vehicle applied its emphasis to saving <u>all</u> sentient beings. This ideal is captured in the Boddhisattva, who vows not to enter "final liberation" until <u>every</u> being is liberated.

It is not only a heart-generous concept, it is completely sound in a practical sense, because it is impossible to live peacefully and freely when others all around you are warlike or enslaved.

Below are the traditional Boddhisattva Vows:

- Sentient beings are numberless. I vow to save them all.
- Buddha-hood is impossible to attain. I vow to attain it.
- May any merit that I generate benefit all sentient beings.

Here is my freely adapted version of the
traditional Bodhisattva Vows:

- Sentient beings are numberless. I
  vow to be of service to them,
  person to person, through my own
  awareness, happiness and loving-
  kindness. (Love, peace, joy—they
  all begin with me; I vow to *be* the
  type of person I want to meet.)

- The Heart of Wonder transcends
  everything. I vow to live in and as the
  Heart of Wonder via the whole
  body-mind.

- All that I do to live happily and
  freely, I dedicate to the happiness
  and freedom of all sentient beings.

Trusting the Heart

(A free rendering of the poem by Sengstan,
Third Zen Patriarch of China)

Life is much easier when you recognize your
opinions as mere opinions.
When you don't cling to or avoid experiences, things
are seen clearly, without disguise.
But when you take surface differences to be
fundamental, the wholeness or completeness of
being seems to split into fragments.

To set up what you like against what you dislike
turns life into war.
To see the single basis of all life, drop your leanings
for or against anything.
When the unified nature of things is not seen, the
heart-mind's peace is disturbed—*to no benefit*!

The Living Condition is vast and complete, like the
open blue sky, without lack or excess. But because
we long for some things and reject others, we do not
see the whole nature of things. To live in wholeness
(holiness) is not to be caught up in outer forms, nor
to be stuck in inner emptiness.

True awakening sees beyond the duality of
"appearances and essence."
Appearances and essence are lovers; each is
transparent to and includes the other.
No need to search for such understanding. Just
abandon your struggling. Give up war!

The more you seek the heart-mind with the thinking-
talking mind, the further you stray from it.
Simply obey the nature of things—your *own* nature!
Already, the heart-mind is entirely present. Hearsay,
beliefs and speculations are of no use. Only *see*.

When you pay attention, moment to moment,
illusions naturally cease.
All dualities are made-up concepts, like unicorns
prancing in the air.
You cannot grasp imaginary unicorns! How silly to
keep trying!
Relax into the wholeness of now, without knowing;
then confusions and contradictions fall away by
themselves.

With clear seeing, the single essence is realized and
entanglements vanish.
Neither "self" nor "other" are taken as ultimately
real.
And not only are such dualities no longer treated as
if they were ultimate—"Oneness" also is understood
to be a mere idea, an object of mind.
In this original openness, free of limit, no description
or comparison applies.

In such wholeness, self-centered struggling is
obsolete. Life is already released; it is self-liberating.
All is empty, clear, self-illuminating, with no exertion
of the intellect. A life of spontaneous faith, trusting
the heart-mind, is born.

To remain in harmony with the wholeness of reality,
clearly remember when doubts and troubles arise:
Not two. In this *Not two*, nothing is excluded.
Nothing is special. Nothing is higher or deeper.
Only *THIS*. No matter where or when,
enlightenment means entering *THIS*.

There is nothing in addition to, or less than, this
present moment of totality. Enlightenment is now
and now and now, forever. Emptiness, freedom,
openness everywhere, while the unending universe
flows on in astounding, precise detail. Infinitely large
and infinitely small; no difference, for definitions and
boundaries have vanished.
All things co-arise and intermingle without
distinction: maggots and butterflies, snakes and
dragons, inextricably mixed up. To live in this
wisdom is to not worry about "perfection."
Trusting the heart-mind is the way of wholeness, for
wholeness is the heart-mind.

Words!
The Way is beyond language.
It is just this timeless presence: No yesterday. No
tomorrow. No today.

The Awakeness of Those Who Are Awake

A Zen student asked her spiritual guide, "What is the enlightenment of the Buddhas?" (This is the same as asking, "What is the awakeness of those who are awake?")

"The enlightenment of the Buddhas," her teacher answered, "is the nature of ordinary awareness."

What *is* the nature of ordinary awareness?

1. **Our real nature is not any knowledge that must be learned.**
    Studying the Pali language, for example, or learning about the "chakra system," is not necessary for <u>directly</u> awakening to our truth. Whatever can be learned (although perhaps valuable, useful and enjoyable) is not identical to the Heart, the Real Person, who is already present and free, depending on nothing.

2. **Our real nature is not anything that is hidden or secret.**
    Being initiated into a secret practice, a secret mantra, a secret text, and so forth, is not

necessary for <u>directly</u> awakening to our truth. Whatever can be kept secret and must be discovered or revealed (although perhaps valuable, useful and enjoyable) is not identical to the Heart, the Real Person, who is already present and free, depending on nothing.

3. **Our real nature is not any experience or state that must be attained.** Archetypal visions, ecstasies of energy, "rising through the lotus of light," and so forth, are not necessary for <u>directly</u> awakening to our truth. Subtle visions,[19] energies, inner lights and other higher psychic phenomena that may occur (although perhaps valuable, useful and enjoyable) are not identical to the Heart, the Real Person, who is already present and free, depending on nothing.

4. **Our real nature is not any body-mind condition that must be held in place.** Manipulating and controlling the body-mind and life-force by intellectual effort, or by celibacy, diet, or yogic practices (such as concentration on energy channels, or continuous prayer, or breathing techniques) are not necessary for <u>directly</u> awakening to our truth. Whatever conditions must be maintained through effort (although perhaps valuable, useful and enjoyable) are not identical to the Heart, the Real Person, who

---

[19] A Zen fable goes: A beginning meditator exclaimed to his teacher in a gush of emotion, "I had a vision of the Buddha, seated on a lotus throne, surrounded by beatific beings!" His teacher replied, "Don't be concerned. Just keep on meditating and such stuff will go away."

is already present and free, depending on nothing.

5. **Our <u>real</u> nature can only be that which <u>is</u> always, already real.**

We are not identical to any object or changing state of the body-mind, no matter how subtle or glorious. Our truth must be the ever-present capacity of all possible states of body and mind, "low" and "high." Our original nature is not bound to time (not a matter of becoming), nor bound to space (not "within" or "without"—indeed, not locatable *anywhere*). Our reality is the Irreducible Mystery that undermines the seeker and all seeking. It is the awakeness of those who are awake, the nature of ordinary awareness, the timeless conscious being, who stands already free as the Heart, the Real Person, depending on nothing.

True Zen is No Zen

Zen, like all true "paths," is obviated by awakening. Like a good doctor, who puts herself out of business by restoring her patients to well-being, all true paths undermine themselves at last and vanish in the light of inherent freedom.

Awakening to real freedom involves a process of shattering our dependency on conventions and limits. That includes dependency on the tradition of Zen. That is why it has been said, "True Zen Is No Zen."

One of the beauties of Zen is that (at its best) it carries a built-in irreverence toward itself. The Buddha himself advised us not to "carry the raft on our shoulders" once we reached the distant shore.

Lao Tzu said, "The Tao is not human-hearted. The sage is not human-hearted." Surely he didn't mean that a sage is a cold-blooded mutant, but that when ego dissolves, formal identity is undone and a wild freedom arises. So we hear Zen wisecracks like, "If you meet the Buddha on the road, kill him." The boldfaced looniness of such remarks is obvious. This is not an instruction to commit murder, but a poke-in-the-ribs at reliance on and attachment to forms.

Of course, transcending a tradition doesn't mean smearing the tradition under your heel. Zen is based on an awakening, which leads to an attitude, which leads to a way of life.

Interestingly, some of what might be thought of as Oriental trappings in the Buddhist traditions are perhaps not Oriental at all, but innate within our species. To wit: decades ago, during a kundalini-driven meditation I spontaneously performed overtone chanting, Gyupta-style. I was intoning sounds, not Tibetan liturgy, but it was multi-chorded singing and it burst forth out of the depths of the blissful wholeness I was feeling.

Also, for a short while I impulsively began the practice of shouting "Ho!" loudly, from my belly, as a way of cutting through reverie to become instantly focused and present. After a few months of doing this, I was reading some thumbnail biographies of Buddhist masters and found that one of them taught the shouting of "Ho!" as a formal practice, and for the same effect.

Lastly, while meditating, my right arm would sometimes rise into a peculiar *mudra* (closed hand, thumb touching forefinger) that I had never seen depicted in any Buddhist artwork or statuary. The mudra held personal power for me, but its meaning is non-verbal, below the mind—best expressed by the mudra itself. About a year after this mudra began to spontaneously appear, I visited the American Museum of Natural History in NYC and saw a wooden statue of Lao-Tzu, his right hand raised in the same mudra.

PART FOUR

The Way of Wonder

ADYASHAKTI

Radical Agnosticism

The Greek word, *gnosis*, means "knowledge," so *agnosis* means "not knowing," and agnosticism means "the way of not knowing." [20] An inquiring heart may lead to genuine agnosticism—which is to say, agnosticism as a spiritual path.

Let's take a deeper look at this path.

As Stephen Batchelor points out in his excellent book, *Buddhism without Beliefs*,[21] the power of the term "agnosticism" has been forgotten. He says it has come to mean not to ask the great questions at all: "To say, 'I don't know,' when you really mean, 'I don't want to know.'"

Agnosticism, then, as it is usually found, is both uninspired and uninspiring. Often it is blended and confused with atheism or nihilism and tends to be just more b.s. (belief systems). In fact, many agnostics are highly-opinionated intellectuals—and what could be more ironic than an agnostic know-it-all?

---

[20] An old pun is that *agnosis* means "not knowing," therefore, *diagnosis* means <u>two</u> people who don't know what's wrong: you and the doctor.

[21] Batchelor, Stephen, *Buddhism Without Beliefs: A Contemporary Guide to Awakening*, Riverhead Books, New York, 1977.

From where I stand, agnosticism is not an excuse for spiritual or moral laziness. My own agnosticism is not really another *ism* or *creed*, but a <u>method</u> or <u>practice</u>; a way of inquiring that deepens my relationship with everything. Such agnosticism is as passionate and challenging as any religious path.

Batchelor reminds us that Thomas Huxley, the British biologist who invented the term "agnostic" in 1869, called it the "agnostic faith." It is the faith or confidence that it is honest and legitimate *to not know*, to not subscribe to a set of rules and meanings; to not, as William James put it, "prematurely close our accounts with reality."

True agnosticism remains intensely loyal to the irreducible mystery of our condition, what Rudolf Otto called the *Mysterium Tremendum et Fascinem*—the tremendous and terrible wonder of the world. But agnosticism as a valid spiritual path is rarely engaged, even by those who claim to be agnostics.

I am an agnostic of the ultimate degree. I could wear a question mark around my neck as religious jewelry. To distinguish my life-way from the dull apathy that passes for agnosticism, I call my path *radical agnosticism*. Not radical as in the French Poodle Liberation Army, but radical as derived from the Latin word *radix*, meaning *at the root*, fundamental, primal.

Agnosticism is radical when one not only does not know any special dogma about God, but, indeed, one does not even know what *knowledge* is.

What is a thought? What is memory? What is consciousness itself?

Where is Earth? Where is space? Where does experience take place?

Where is the boundary between myself and the world and you?

When is time? When is now?

I, for one, do not know. I confess, with my whole heart, my whole body: I really don't know. I don't know what I am, or what you are. I am simply <u>being</u> what I am altogether, without clinging to body and mind as if any part or function or experience is a final identity.

Consider this: There is a world of difference between being able to name or describe something: a thought, a dream, a memory—a maple tree, apple tree, rhinoceros tree—and knowing what that thing or event or experience IS. Likewise, measuring the properties of a thing—mass and chemical makeup and so forth—is absolutely not the same as knowing what it *is*. Nor does knowing how something works—that phosphorus combusts spontaneously in contact with oxygen—amount to knowing what it *is*.

It doesn't matter what language is used to represent experience—from Hieroglyphics to English to advanced mathematics; and it doesn't matter through what lens one perceives the universe—through shamanism or sexuality or astrophysics—one still cannot objectively know the wonder that is experience *itself.* Existence *itself.* Consciousness *itself.* This is our amazing condition, this present and Perfect Mystery. Unique, incomparable, indefinable, illimitable.

To behave like know-it-alls just because we have highly developed languages and sciences and arts—all of which are mere symbols or descriptions of reality—is an arrogance that would be laughable, were it not so harmful. We've confused our own symbols and abstractions with real life, like mistaking the red lines on a map for the highways.

"How far is Chicago from New York?"

"Oh"—holding up thumb and forefinger—"about this far."

Evelyn Underhill, a great mystic of the past century, cautioned against this basic error of misidentifying reality with mere perception:

> This sense-world, this seemingly real external universe, though useful and valid in other respects, cannot be the world, but only the self's picture of it. It is a work of art, not a scientific fact; and whilst it may possess the profound significance proper to great works of art, very slight investigation shows that it is a picture whose relationship to reality is at best symbolic and approximate, and which would have no meaning for selves whose senses, or channels of communication, happen to be arranged upon a different plan. The evidence of the senses then, cannot be accepted as evidence of the nature of ultimate reality.

Ordinary folks, too, have come to understand this liberating wonder. Years ago, I wrote a newspaper article called *The Opposing Side of Euthanasia*—about spouses who choose to care for someone until "death us do part." One of the persons I interviewed was a retired economics professor who was 74 at the time and had just spent a couple years caring for his dying wife. He said something that has always stuck with me:

"For most of my life I fought against mystery, thinking that answers were available and I could obtain them. I don't feel that way any longer. Now I'm comfortable with mystery, I'm reconciled with my own fundamental ignorance."

Giving ourselves permission to not know can open us to what the 14th-Century German mystic Meister Eckhart called "Divine Ignorance." He taught that such unknowing is our essential condition—not caused by sin or anything else—but uncaused, innate and immutable. Clearly, then, this native condition is not a temporary lack of knowledge (such as not knowing a cure for cancer) that may be resolved in the future by further research and information. Rather, our eternal situation is the inability to grasp the ungraspable, the mystery of our true identity, which is prior to and beyond all learning.

The Nobel-laureate quantum physicist, Werner Heisenberg, recognized this principle when he said, "All cognition must be seen as formed over an abyss."

What would happen—what would it feel like—to let go of all our hand-holds, our foot-holds, our mind-holds, and leap into that abyss? Has anyone ever done this? Is the leap survivable with sanity intact?

Indeed, I have made the leap myself. So have numerous other mystics across many cultures and times and places. (And my pet rock tells me that I'm still relatively sane.) Listen to what this surrender felt like to the 10th Century Greek Orthodox Christian, St. Symeon, the New Theologian:

> The more a man enters the light of understanding, the more aware he is of his own ignorance. And when the light reveals itself fully and unites with him and draws him into itself, so that he finds himself alone in a sea of light, then he is emptied of all knowledge and immersed in absolute unknowing.

By now, you may be thinking, "And this is good news?" Actually, it is wonderful news: This contemplation of Mystery has the power to liberate us from the phony bonds of all our concepts, opinions, judgments, memories (the "past"); from all limited identities superimposed on Life As It Nakedly IS. Our awareness opens into a vast, free space that allows room for the life-force[22] to flow and play. But because Eckhart's term "Ignorance" suggests negative connotations, I prefer to call this awakening, "Deep Wonder."

Practicing Deep Wonder brings on a crisis in consciousness, where words and thoughts fail and the independent self ("the knower") capitulates. The grace of dis-illusionment shines in such moments of utter honesty. The scaffolding of the self-construct no longer holds up, and one falls helpless into the Heart of the Divine. Then one lives <u>as</u> Reality, not through knowing, but through natural surrender.

Having pointed to the liberating principle of our inherent Mystery, I must emphasize that Deep Wonder is not at odds with education and knowledge. PLEASE HEAR THIS: I am a lifelong student and a huge fan of the natural sciences and the humanities—I am not anti-learning!

As an evangelist for wonder, I would never encourage anyone to abandon learning or critical thinking. Wonder and learning are lovers. Indeed, this path is not suited to anyone who does not have the ability to think and feel intelligently for oneself.

---

[22] In Eastern traditions, this emancipation of latent energy in the body-mind is called "the awakening of *kundalini*." But descriptions of currents of radiant life-energy flowing in the body-mind can be found in every tradition.

Deep Wonder (radical agnosticism) does not mean "anything goes," just as encouraging a wide-open mind is not to suggest that your brains should spill out in your lap! Such freedom is for Mature Audiences Only. [23]

Radical agnosticism can be summed in the profound confession: "What I <u>Am</u> is beyond all knowing." This declaration expresses awe, not feeble-mindedness. It is an epistemological statement—that is, it refers to the structure of knowledge, which in turn, refers to the structure of the universe. Just as the eyes cannot see themselves, consciousness cannot become a separate object to itself, in order to know itself.

In other words, we can't draw a circle around our existence and define it, because there is no distance, no independent platform from which to view our total being and process. Thus, the real Self is not identical to anything perceived by the bodily senses or conceived by the thinking mind, because such are mere objects to awareness. Our True Identity always remains unqualified, pure capacity; it never becomes a "something." Everyone already <u>is</u> the Perfect Mystery, Consciousness Itself, Totality, God.

So all that stuff you assumed *is* the real you? (Female, 40ish, tall, overweight, Hispanic, shy, college-educated, etc.) It's all only surface functioning—a moving wave upon the ocean of your real identity. What you <u>are</u> at Heart includes every level of functioning: body, mind, soul and spirit. So

---

[23] Remember the Heaven's Gate cultists who killed themselves in order to be transported to a Hale-Bopp spaceship (after packing clothes for their discarded bodies!)? Those blighted souls displayed defective reasoning, not wonder. We cannot afford to be fools about this business of life.

to identify only with the body or mind is to forget the vastness of Whole Being. When you awaken to your real nature, it blows the lid off this reductionist image of yourself, forever.

Radical agnosticism unfetters the being from bogus self-images and brings clear seeing. But it does not offer an alternative set of meanings and beliefs to replace the ones it flushes away. It is not consoling. And nothing is glossed over: not sorrow, not pain, not death. At the same time, it leads one to intuit our limitless, Original Nature—so open and empty it both inspires and sucks one's breath away.

Therefore: I don't know. You don't know. Neither did Gautama, the Buddha. Neither does the President of the United States. Nor will the citizens of the farthest-flung future civilization. Life will never stop living so that we can pin it down, own and control it. And I, for one, am thrilled to let life be greater than all my knowing. I am willing to live at infinity with an uncovered heart.

If you feel moved to taste this freedom (to "Drink the Ganges in a single gulp"), then just see clearly that, already, in this moment, you do not know what a single thing *is*.

Now abide in this sheer truth and never forsake its amazement.

The Way of Wonder

I had a very dear friend named Marilyn who had reached the last stanza of the poem of her life. Cancer was rapidly destroying her body. When I visited her just before her death, Marylyn asked her son and me to carry the coffin a friend had crafted for her into her bedroom so she could see it.

"Ooh, it's beautiful!" she said. "He did a great job."

That's the kind of person she was. Flowing with the River that carried her into birth and swept her on, into death. No angry thrashing, resisting the current. Well, maybe at times a little thrashing…

Old Man River, he just keeps rollin'. He don't say nothin'.

Sometimes, when the pain got bad, she felt afraid.

But Old Man River, he just keeps rollin' along.

Marilyn did tell me she wished she had lived all her days in the way she lived them toward the end. No time for pettiness. Why did she ever trouble with little things at all? No time left for anything but present astonishment at the living world.

How many times have you heard this very theme? Dozens of times—*hundreds* of times? Same with me. Yet coming from Marilyn, it struck me anew. She had always been a wise, loving person with a wealth of humor and the ability to bring out the best in nearly everyone she met. She had already been living her life in a vital, intense way. This, even though she had broken her back in a toboggan accident twelve years earlier and had since been paralyzed from the waist down. But even such a brightly alive personality had learned to clarify and simplify her presence. Taste the whole ocean in the salty teardrop of *this moment*.

How can the rest of us go about doing this? Is there a teaching that can help awaken us in this day-to-day theater of life and open us to live it more freely and fully?

I believe there is. It is the teaching of Wonder.

The teaching of Wonder can be brought into focus with one simple question:

DO YOU *KNOW* WHAT ANYTHING *IS?*

The question is so childlike that it is easy to miss its profundity. But honestly, my sisters and brothers, from the sky of your mind to the furnace of your belly: Do you *know* what anything *is?*

To help illumine this question, I shall quote at length from a novel, *Ember from the Sun*. The characters in the following scene are Mike, a young, Anglo high school teacher; and Old Man[24], a Native American medicine man from the (apocryphal) Quanoot tribe.

> The two sat in silence. Mike
> liked this beautiful old Quanoot,
> whether he understood him or not.
> It seemed to him that the shaman

---

[24] One might recall that the Chinese name of the founder of Taoism, Lao Tzu, means "Old Man."

was wrapped in an invisible robe of peace, yet he did not seem monk-like, withdrawn. His eyes shined; his body was relaxed; Old Man was at home in the world.

"Tell me how you got to be...you know...the way you are today," Mike said.

"Like all of us, I was born this way," Old Man said. "But I soon forgot my nature and it took a while to return to it.

"My father was an Anglican missionary, from London; my mother was one of his schoolgirls. He had a wife back in England, so my parents never wed, but he took a liking to me and made me his altar boy. He filled my head with Protestant dogma and English literature, while my grandmother filled my head with Quanoot-cha and all her old tales.

"In those days, when a boy reached his twelfth winter, it was time to go into the deep woods and wait for his guardian spirit to come. He would fast and wander, and bathe in the manner we did today, except in icy streams. After days and nights, he would fall into a delirium and a spirit would enter him in the form of a bird, or a wolf, or whatever, and teach him his own magic song and spirit dance, and give him guidance to learn the skills of canoe maker, hunter, or fisherman, when he returned to the village."

"Career counseling," Mike said.

Old Man nodded.

"What spirit came to you?"

"That first winter, nothing. My head was filled with conflicting beliefs. I almost died from hunger. My uncles came and found me and carried me home. So I decided to specialize. The second winter, I focused on Christianity and its teachings."

"And?"

"It did not fit, and I realized for me it had never fit. So the third winter, I abandoned such notions and devoted myself only to Quanoot-cha."

"What happened?"

"I could not get past the feeling that it, too, did not fit. Quanoot-cha was in my ears, but not in my marrow. I had not been afraid the first two winters, not even when I was starving, but then I became terrified. I had nothing to believe in, not a jot of truth. I didn't know the right way, and now I had lost the only ways I knew. Now I was nobody at all, a total failure.

"How could I endure such hollowness?" Old Man said. "I decided to die, to fast until death, since I was already starving.

"So I climbed over the top of a mountain ridge and followed a valley stream, until I overlooked a steep-walled rock canyon, where a waterfall spilled into a deep green pool. I sat down on a large rock shelf. 'A perfect place to die,' I told myself, and I breathed out with my whole spirit, surrendering everything. I became so relaxed I think I swayed like a leaf.

"A kingfisher rattled on a nearby perch. I saw the biggest trout I have ever seen leap out of the rapids below. The mist and blow from the falls chilled my face and ruffled my hair; and the air was lush with the smell of clear, cold water. Then the sun broke through the clouds and a rainbow arced through the spray. So far, dying was beautiful.

"Next, I had to pee. So I stepped to the ledge and added my little stream to the roaring cascade.

Old Man's eyes crinkled into a smile.

"All at once I understood the joke. And I started to laugh, and I laughed so hard I almost slipped off the ledge."

Mike chuckled. "The joke?"

"The waterfall," he said. "It was like the mighty, gushing flow of life itself, and my tiny stream seemed to me like the concepts that we add to it. We try to make meaning, a philosophy, something to believe in—because we're afraid. We refuse to dive in. We know the mighty current will sweep us away and that will be the end of our little selves. I had been tormenting myself, trying to sum up everything, to turn life into a conclusion, and suddenly my struggle was laughable. It was my recoil from mystery, the river of life."

"It was plain that I did not know what anything is. That was the simple truth. The trees, the canyon, the crashing water, the cold mist—I had no way to interpret any of it. It was all naked wonder. And the feeling dissolved me with such force that I suddenly knew I really *would* die, for I had no way to hold on to the world or to myself.

"The knot in my heart flew open and I passed beyond all knowing. And there I stood: stark, free...*whole*...breathing down to the tips of my toes."

Mike felt a tingling over his skin. Old Man's joy was contagious. He seemed even now to be the teen-aged boy who had come unraveled in beauty.

"You're saying, 'Truth is within'," Mike said.

"That sounds like something Jesus said, not me."

"Then truth is in the things that you accomplish in this world? The good that you do?"

"That sounds like Quanoot-cha."

Mike knit his brow. "I don't get it."

"Neither do I get it. I have never grasped it." Old Man waved his fingers and hands and arms in graceful, swirling waves. "There are no handholds in a waterfall. No footholds. I don't own the life power, I go with it, wherever it takes me."

"And it guided you to become a shaman."

"Yes, and so I am, even still."

A process very much like this actually happened to me when I was a teen-ager. In a timeless instant, I awakened, just as the old medicine man describes, into the open space of original nature—an awareness without center or bounds. I've been a devotee of that freedom ever since. Sometimes that makes me appear stupid, because nearly everyone else seems to know with certainty truths that I don't know at all.

For example: Religious creationists *know* the truth of Genesis with self-assured conviction, while orthodox Darwinists come off as equally smug. Such self-satisfaction from both camps, it seems to me, lacks humility before mystery. As if there is not more to the living cosmos than is inked in the pages of *any* book: *The Holy Bible* or *The Origin of Species*. As if the horizon-less ocean of existence can be reduced to some island speck of local, mortal experience.

"Vanity of vanities," sayeth the preacher, "All is vanity."

Therefore, regarding religious dogma: If your mind rejects reason, or if it has bought into a self-defining, closed system of pseudo-reason—what might be called "reasonable nonsense"—then you invent for yourself phony limitations. You lock the universe in a prison of your own design. Reject critical thinking and you are like a naïve child, exploitable by every kind of cult. You are blocking the power of knowledge that can free you from superstition. And all that you fear defines and controls you.

Also, regarding scientific dogma: If your life view is uncomfortable with the unknowable, afraid of the infinite—and you hurry to fill in glimpses of the abyss with facts and images from the latest grasp of science, then you invent for yourself phony limitations. You lock the universe in a prison of your own design. You are blocking the spiritual awakening that undermines the knower. And all that you fear defines and controls you.

In short, those who reject reason and science tend to be intellectually undeveloped, like little children; and those who reject mystery tend to be dry and rigid, like old fogies. Both personality types are stunted, incomplete. And their potential for love, wisdom and happiness is incomplete.

Therefore, the way of Wonder that I recommend does not support pre-rational and magical thinking—the stuff of the superstitions of the ages. Nor does it idolize the discursive mind and encyclopedic knowledge as the proper vehicles of truth. It encourages neither fools nor know-it-alls.

To further explain this way of Wonder—the path of the intuition of Mystery—I need to contrast its weak and strong aspects.

The Weak Wonder Principle (or what might be called "superficial wonder") says: "Based on all the facts that we know about it, isn't life amazing?" For example, knowing about atoms, molecules, proteins, cells, tissues, organs and organ systems, isn't the human body wonderful?

Every reader will be familiar with the Weak Wonder Principle. It's the force that drives our information cult, fueled by entertainment media, such as the Discovery Channel. "Hey, Mabel! Did you know that a giraffe has a *blue* tongue? And it's a foot and a half long! And its tongue and lips are prehensile! *Look* at that! Like Mick Jagger!"

The Weak Wonder Principle is a lot of fun. It's the feeling of, *Wow! Who'd a Thunk it!*[25] This

---

[25] There is even a Very Weak Wonder Principle, in which people need to resort to belief in UFOs, angel visitations, magic healing crystals, the Lost Continent of Atlantis, and so on, as evidence that life is wonderful. As if natural life—the perfume of a rose, the stink of shit—isn't astounding enough.

approach to life often sees the natural world as a treasure chest full of amazing material objects waiting to be discovered, sorted by name or number, and put to good use. All that we presently do not know has simply not yet been found out.

Follow the path of superficial wonder and you can become a walking storehouse of information—say, an Isaac Asimov—who at his death had written more than 470 books, surpassing any other Earthling. Great stuff. I've read a couple dozen of his books myself. But all that knowledge—while perhaps useful—won't necessarily be *transformative*. Superficial wonder won't take you beyond *yourself* as the *knower* of all this cool stuff. You will not transcend your scope of information, your particular frame of reference. And no matter how modern and up-to-date your box is, no matter its dimensions, it's still a prison. Why? Because mere information is not, in itself, the realization of the nature of reality. Nor does information lead, necessarily, to the simplest change of heart.

Yet information (especially scientific knowledge) is the golden calf of modern culture. Indeed, a common misreading of science—an error too often propagated by scientists themselves—is that scientific inquiry offers an *alternative* to the Mystery of our existence. According to this view, our choice is to remain uninformed—and therefore, to regard the cosmos as fundamentally mysterious and beyond our control—or to find out what everything is, how it works and how it came to be (through the observational and analytical powers of modern science)—and thereby to get a handle on how to predict and control everything. Even the weather. Even death.

But it strikes me as odd when scientifically-inclined people are slow to grasp the punch line of quantum physics, which has shown that all

knowledge and experience is localized and *relative*.
Nobel-winning physicists, like Heisenberg and Bohr,
and not just religious ecstatics like Meister Eckhart
and Rumi, have proclaimed the same condition: that
we *cannot* attain ultimate knowledge of the cosmos,
or even a carrot.

"There is no absolute knowledge," wrote
Jacob Bronowski, the late mathematician and author
of *The Ascent of Man*. "All information is imperfect.
We have to treat it with humility."

Bronowski asks us to consider that scientists
are *not* mere scribes, copying down objective facts
which lie hidden like Easter eggs, waiting to be
found. Scientists are more akin to artists, describing
and structuring the world as they see it. And what
they see is not separable from what they bring to the
observation.

"For order is not there for the mere
looking," he wrote. "There is no way of pointing a
finger or a camera at it. Order must be discovered
and, in a deep sense, it must be *created*."

Bronowski points out that the portraits
scientists create do not *fix* the world, they only
explore it. Each new line may enhance the image, but
never makes it final. He summarizes this idea
poignantly: "We seek truth, but what we find is
knowledge and what we fail to find is certainty."

So now we come to the *Strong* Wonder
Principle—or what could rightly be called Deep
Wonder: the revelation of Mystery that springs up as
profound emotion, not from the "wowing" intellect
but from the ocean floor of the feeling heart. Yet the
religious ecstatics throughout history—those whose
lives are on fire with Deep Wonder—have had
relatively little to say about it. Not that they wouldn't
shout their epiphanies from the highest hilltops if
only they could—but words and meanings have been
permanently outdistanced by direct insight. The

thinking mind capitulates; the independent knower is undone; the separate one melts into the whole bright sky of silence. In exasperation, the poor mystic, beside herself to communicate her joy, winds up talking about what the Mystery is <u>not</u> ("Not anything you can perceive with the bodily senses; not anything you can conceive with the thinking mind.") because she cannot reduce to words what it <u>IS</u>! Deep Wonder belongs only to those who have broken through the multi-level Chinese boxes of <u>all</u> their knowledge and conditioning, to enter the freedom of perfect, original Mystery.[26]

The Chinese emperor asked the enlightened Buddhist sage, Bodhidharma, "Who are you?"

The sage replied, "I do not know."

Deep Wonder outshines the limits of information, and communes with the universe at source and depth, as profound Mystery. This principle has the power to distill the mind to its own naked essence. The mind comes to rest in the Heart of Unknowing—what the Old Testament calls "the peace that surpasses understanding"—and from that orientation the newborn woman or man is able to freely live and die.

It is important to understand that nothing that I have said above should be interpreted as anti-intellectual. I am myself a huge fan of learning, and I certainly encourage everyone to pursue a lifelong education—sciences <u>and</u> humanities—and to learn how to think critically. Deep Wonder—the intuition

---

[26] Other names for this inherent freedom are: **don't-know mind, beginner's mind, no-mind** (Zen), **uncarved block, unbleached silk** (Taoism), **unknowing** (Christian mystics), *shunyata* (Sanskrit = "void"), *mosshoryo* (Japanese = "unthinkable, unspeakable"), **freedom from the known** (Jiddu Krishnamurti), **divine ignorance** (Meister Eckhart), **the open secret** (Rumi).

of the inherent Mystery of our being—is not *against* knowledge, it is simply *beyond* knowledge: our Mystery is greater than all present and all <u>possible</u> information.

In my living room, I have a foot-tall bronze statue of Andreas Vesalius, the 16th-Century Flemish anatomist, who created the first accurate, detailed anatomy of the human body (and thereby dispelled a mountain of medieval nonsense taken from the Greek physician, Galen, which had been taught as medicine for three-hundred years). Vesalius represents to me the analytical-logical realm, the best of natural sciences, humanism, scholarship and critical thinking.

I also have a bronze statue of Shakti, consort of Shiva. In Hindu mysticism, Shiva represents the irreducibly mysterious singularity of Consciousness itself—the Absolute. Shakti is the Goddess-Mother of eternal energy and delight, creatrix of all the worlds. These two are enfolded in eternal embrace—a timeless dialectic—which might best be described as the Divine Logos (Spirit/Mind) making love with the Divine Eros (Nature/Body). For me, the Shakti statue represents the intuitive realm, the wellspring of dreams, music, art, poetry, religion, romance and ecstasy.

It is not only possible, it is <u>necessary</u> for each of us to live a faith that engages body, mind and spirit; a lifeway that draws from worldly <u>and</u> transcendental wisdom. One can only fly on both wings.

The Absolute Signal of Being

1) While every possibility of experience comes and goes, Bright Mystery remains. Uncaused. Timeless. Immutable. Indestructible. Mystery is the Heart, and the Heart is Radiant— forever shining as all worlds.

2) When the Mystery is strongly intuited and felt, the Radiance—the dynamic force of the Heart—begins to move in the body. A spontaneous release of power flows through the subtle channels of the multi-dimensional human vehicle. The current is <u>heard</u> (as harmonic sound), <u>seen</u> (as radiant light) and <u>felt</u> (as blissful force) as it flows in a living circuit throughout the body-mind.

3) Mystery, when fully felt (to the final degree of ego-dissolution) outshines the limits of all that is known or can ever be known. Such outshining is initiation into ultimate freedom.

4) Until such initiation, the Mystery remains an idea, a symbol, an abstract object, a thing apart (and sought after). After initiation, all the myriad qualities of experience cannot mask this Absolute Signal of Being. Thus, the

awakened one intuits and lives unqualified life, presently, even in the ordinary forms of the world.

5) As the nagging sense of limitation and dilemma vanishes from mind, spiritual seeking (or all motivation toward escape) becomes obsolete. An awakened person is not looking for release, but already free. Therefore, upon enlightenment, there is nothing left to be, but present and whole; and nothing left to do, but take care of the moment now at hand.

Feeling the Mystery

1. All knowledge is secondary, it merely knows *about*; it depends upon and incompletely reflects whole existence itself. Knowing about the myriad stuff that appears never can amount to or "catch up" to what always, already IS.

2. Knowing cannot apprehend what is prior to the faculty of knowing. Consciousness cannot grasp its own identity. Therefore, Consciousness Itself is never identified, never known, never seen, never objectified, but only <u>understood</u> as Mystery—only intuited and presumed and lived as the Heart of everything.

3. Enlightenment is radical intuition, not objective knowing. It is <u>being</u>, not seeing.

4. Presume this Mystery as the very condition of all that arises and never falsely identify with anything. Recognize that all that appears is forever included in and transcended by the Unknowable which is Whole and Indivisible, Indestructible and Irreducible. Understand that the Real

Condition is not limited to any of the appearing conditions, within or without.

5. Presume the Perfect Mystery (Native Wonder) and live. Within this Mystery, everything appears and changes and disappears. That which is the Source and Support of all things and events is forever unthreatened. The Source is Unknowable (as Object, or objective information) yet obvious as one's own nature.

6. *In relation to the physical body* the intuitive thrill of inherently free Being is <u>felt</u> in the chest; thus the Bright Mystery is also named the Heart.

The Great Questions

It is each person's responsibility to directly investigate all the hearsay about spirit and truth and enlightenment, in order to discover the reality for oneself. To this end, questions are the builders, not the saboteurs, of a realized faith or life-way. The courage to question demonstrates faith—faith in one's own process, faith in the hero's journey.

Of course, not all questions arise from the same depth. I was taught in journalism school that every article should attempt to cover the *five W's and one H*: Who? What? When? Where? Why? How? But those questions only lead to information—"Just the facts, ma'am." They are not the great questions, which may lead to wisdom.

Science offers an endless supply of conundrums to solve: Why do cells age? How much of human behavior depends on genes? Of what is dark matter composed? Is there an ultimate elementary particle? Is there intelligent life beyond Earth? Are men from Mars and women from Venus? And on and on—tempting mysteries of biology, cosmology and physics waiting to be unveiled; and, of course, the answers will spawn a new generation of questions, and a new line of beneficial and frightful technologies.

But again, most of these are not the great questions, the perennial questions that have haunted humankind through the ages. Just a century ago, no one had even heard of dark matter, subatomic particles, and so forth.

These questions and their answers don't reach down to what Zen Buddhists call *kokoro*—the heart-mind. Kokoro means all one's powers of awareness: the bodily senses, intellect, emotional intelligence, intuition. A question that grabs you in your heart-mind gets you where you *live*.

I asked the psychologist Sam Keen—years ago, when he was writing *Hymns to an Unknown God*—what he considered to be the great questions. He said they are the very ones that myths and religions address:

- Who am I?
- Where did the world and I come from? Where am I going?
- What is the meaning of my life, my death?
- What are my gifts? What is my vocation? What may I give my life to?
- What must I do to die with a sense of completeness?
- What do I *really* want? What can I hope for?
- What do I fear?
- Who are my heroes? My people?
- How was I wounded? How can I be healed? How do I forgive?
- Who have I hurt?
- What is my shadow?
- What is evil? Why does evil exist? What is *my* relationship to evil?
- What is sacred, inviolable?
- What is taboo?
- How can I help others?

That's Keen's list, and certainly, it can be added to. Listen to the question the Hindu poet Kabir asks, "O Tell me: Who have you loved your whole life long?"

That is a powerful query! It reminds me of a Hasidic tale of a poor woodsman who fell in love with the King's daughter when he came upon her bathing in a river. He declared his love to her with such passion and sincerity she was moved to tears. "Lover, it is only in the cemetery that I will one day be able to join with you," she said, meaning that only in death can a princess and a woodsman become equals. Nevertheless, the young man, beside himself with adoration, took her words literally and went to the cemetery to wait for the princess to appear.

Day after day, as he waited, he thought of nothing but his beloved, contemplating her lovely form and qualities. This led him to feel grateful to her ancestors, who had made possible her birth, and to meditate on all the elements that supported her life. His appreciation expanded to include vaster spheres of being that gave life to the woman he loved, until, at last, it seemed to him that the One who was his Beloved was the very universe itself.

"O tell me: Who have you loved your whole life long?"

During our childhoods, we rehearse a set of official answers to the great questions that are given to us by our families, in church, in school, the army, the workplace, books and movies. However, what leads us to authentic adulthood is not having memorized the answers, but living with the profound questions.

To be spoon-fed the answers to the great questions betrays the possibility of discovering truth. To illustrate: If I had been raised Catholic and had been made to memorize the catechism on the purpose of life, "The purpose of life is to know, love and serve God," I might have revolted from that doctrine, just as I did rebel from my own Jewish schooling. But, having lived with the great question ("What is the purpose of my life?"), I have come to *my* answer, *my* truth; and now I can proclaim that the purpose of my life is—to know, love and serve God.

Yes, that is exactly my life's purpose, but I found it for myself—and the God I'm talking about won't fit between the covers of a book, or within the bounds of any belief system—nor even fit inside my own mind.

This is why in the Zen tradition it is said, "Enlightenment cannot be passed from father to son." In other words, it cannot be inherited. It cannot be taught. Enlightenment refers to a profound awakening that can only be realized directly and then lived.

To ask the great questions is not optional. There is no way finally to avoid asking them. Sure, we can ignore them for a while—there are many distractions in life. Nevertheless, eventually these questions enforce themselves because they are real. As Sam Keen put it, "I didn't make them up."

Old age, disease, death, tragedy, beauty, love, glory, joy; we must be reconciled with our experience. Someone might protest, "I don't have time for these questions. I'm no philosopher. I've got to live my life." Okay, so live your life—until the world clobbers you—until you get cancer, or your child dies, or you realize you haven't the slightest idea who you are and you can't figure it out from the diplomas on your wall, the stack of plastic in your wallet, or the type of car you drive.

Keen warns that the longer we defer the investigation of what is centrally important to us and continue with a life that is largely uninspected, the more traumatic the turnaround is apt to be. Some of us have to edge very close to dying in order to come alive again, to get <u>real</u>. But the earlier we sincerely ask these great questions, the more the answers will be integrated with our lives and the better chance we have of making choices as we go along that don't turn out to be disastrous.

Joseph Campbell, the mythologist, wrote about "the hero's journey", which is shorthand for this whole process of delving beneath one's day-to-day persona to seek abiding truth. Going down into the strangeness of our own lives—finding out what moves us. In the heroic journey, we leave the familiar world in which we have been indoctrinated with readymade conclusions and we seek our own experience and learn to tell our own stories.

Odysseus returned; Jason returned; all successful heroes return. They bring back with them a boon: They no longer talk out of someone else's experience. They are not like the Pharisees; they are not quoting Page 158, Section 34 of the handbook. They have become self-realized, and therefore, *disillusioned* and unexploitable; and they are tolerant and supportive of the quests and questions of others.

Zero = One = Infinity

Know-it-alls fear the abyss, the death of the knower (the would-be controller). But in the intoxication of love and trust, the mystic *groks* that Zero is not the terrifying annihilator, but Pure Capacity in which all things appear and are accomplished.

Zero (Emptiness, Void, Origin, Plenum) is open and unqualified and permits time, space, energy and matter to freely arise as ever-flowing permutations of itself.

The humor of awakening holds onto nothing, for all things are sacrificial worship and realization of Source, which is forever empty (unformed, unqualified) and free. In the crazy-wise language of Buddhism: "Form is Emptiness; Emptiness is Form."

This paradox also can be expressed as a "crazy" mathematical equation: Zero = One = Infinity.

At the interface of Zero (the <u>uncreated</u> field of all potentiality) and Infinity (the manifest cosmos of space-time-energy-matter) arises the unique One ("I", the emergent and temporary personality or ego-soul). "I" (body-mind-soul) am equal to (continuous with) Everything and Nothing. The universe unfolds moment by moment—and endless changes are played out in the grand theater of life.

Already, there is no *thing* (no limit) at all. You can look everywhere, within and without, but you'll never find any "box" that contains what IS.

There is no box. No limitation. Reality cannot be reduced to locatable, objective thing-ness. It cannot be found (or lost). The Real Condition is always fluid, open-ended, total and mysterious.

Experience is not a dream. It is real enough. Within the phenomenal dimension, if a speeding Mack truck hits you, it will squash you flat. But experience is *similar* to a dream, in that it has no ultimate implications. Things have no absolute substance; changes have no eternal effect. Fall into the Zero of the heart and the imaginary box (the dreamlike stream of knowing) loses its weightiness, its solidness, its power to define.

We are not bound by any size, or shape, or image, or word, or world. *We are not things.* We are beyond dimension, beyond identification. All identities are false. Already, there is no dilemma, no need to escape, for we are not confined, but free.

You Cannot Grasp, but You Can __BE__

What led, in my case, to ego-dissolution and awakening, was practicing for a couple decades the very precise honesty of *not knowing*. In meditation, whenever anything—thought, emotion, sensation— appeared, I inquired deeply "What *IS* it?" or, simply, "What *IS*?" After some practice, the question became condensed to "*What?*"

I did not verbally ask these questions over and over, like a mantra, but rather, *felt* with all my being into the mystery of existence itself. Less frequently, I would practice the more traditional self-inquiry (as taught by Ramana Maharshi and Nisargadatta Maharaj): "Who *am* I?" or, "Who is *aware* of this?" or most simply, "*Who?*"

Another version of self-enquiry is to ask "Where?" (*Where* is this experience arising? *Where* is the self-idea? *Where* is a thought? *Where* is the body? *Where* is any sense of location?)

This method of inquiry leads to deep abiding at the Heart—the root mystery of our being. It leads beyond conceptualizing, imagining, abstracting, objectifying and reifying experience. In other words, it leads beyond the dream of knowing to the bright void of original being. Then, whatever appears within that luminous freedom is seen in its naked suchness—undistorted by interpretations and meanings. All experience then remains unbrokenly whole, not fragmented, and transparent to the freedom of the Heart. As they say in Zen, "The clouds do not hinder the vast sky, nor does a barking dog disturb the moon."

Ego is a construct. Not-knowing is de-constructive. Ultimately, through awareness and practice of the simple, natural honesty of not-knowing, the self-construct is undermined and awareness "expands" or "returns" to original freedom and clarity.

To plumb the original depth, it is necessary to trust your own essence to the degree of perfect letting go of mind, self, the "knower" and all knowing. You must be willing to fall into the abyss, to let go with *both* hands. It takes real trust to allow the ego-dissolution to occur.

"I" died, and it was not annihilation. This is not surprising, because "I" disappears every night in deep sleep and reappears every morning. When "I" disappears and only deep, dreamless awareness remains, it is called *nirvana*. Upon realizing such liberation from the limitation of "I", consciousness no longer identifies with the "I"-sense, but recognizes it for what it is—not a concrete entity, but rather a program for organizing experience and information.

"I" comes and goes. It is only a cognition and does not exist as an independent self. Everything comes and goes. There are no everlasting objects. As the Ch'an master Hui Neng used to say, "Not one thing!"

No thing in the flow of life lasts. What *is* everlasting is the source of life. Moreover, the source of life and the flow of life are one, just as an ocean and its waves are one. Without the support of the ocean, no waves arise. Following this metaphor, all the worlds are the manifest waves of the ocean of conscious being. Therefore, there is nothing you can do about the way it *IS*, but relax and go with the flow.

The Mystery Is Not Mysterious

The Mystery is not mysterious. Not hidden, vague, dark or obscure. Yes, the Mystery is a Perfect Secret that can never be reduced to mere information. However, this Secret is not <u>hidden</u>! The Secret is only Open, or always, already <u>Revealed</u>. The Secret is ever-present, complete, bright and obvious. Already, no one knows what a single thing *is*. Mystery is our native condition. It is not the result of anything, and it is not a condition we must earn or acquire.

Part of the problem of "getting to" enlightenment is the very presumption that it involves distance or return, as if the purpose of life is to return to its source. But how could life continue for an instant if it were separated from its source? Enlightenment involves the living of another presumption: that Source and Life are always, already indivisibly <u>whole</u>.

Another of the barriers to enlightenment (and the most widespread error throughout all mystic paths) is the notion that reality lies *within*. This implies that to go within, to turn attention *inward*, is to move <u>toward</u> truth, to be heading in the "God-ward" direction. But, in fact, there is no God-ward direction! "Within" is no more absolute than "without." To seek in any direction is to turn away.

Seekers who turn within, hunting happiness, become complicated, solemn and uptight. Seekers who turn without, hunting happiness, become scattered in a thousand directions.

Why this turning? Why the seeking? What presumptions are being dramatized by all the strategies of the search? Since reality is not a thing, a person, a force, an object of body or mind, how can it be located by searching for it?

All the while, truth is only whole. Truth is totally present now. Struggling to attain our innate nature "someday" (when you finally get holy enough, non-neurotic enough, knowledgeable enough, slim enough) ignores our innate abundance in <u>this</u> timeless moment.

What if the seeking heart came to REST? Not searching, not grasping at all. Not pretending to own or know or control. In that deep surrender, the mystery and its freedom become obvious, and consciousness stands nakedly present and unbounded. And that simple, intimate presence IS love and happiness and completeness (enlightenment).

There is only mystery, but there is nothing mysterious about the mystery. The mystery is as plain as the vast blue sky. The wonder of existence is not hidden or removed. Not even subtle. It is more intimate than our heartbeat. It really could not be more obvious! Already, in your present experience, without adding or subtracting a thing, you simply do not know what anyone or anything *is*. You do <u>not</u> know what you are (so stop imagining and pretending; quit burdening yourself with phony identities).

Typically, we draw back from the on-flowing gush of life to figure out who we are and what it all is. We withdraw emotionally, energetically, bodily. Wanting to avoid this appearance, hold on to that one. Wishing to know and control everything, in order to be safe from relationship and change and death—all threats to the separate "self."

But already there is not a definable, isolatable, locatable, circumscribable, independent self. Instead, the sense of difference, separation and independence *springs from our own act of withdrawal.* In other words, the separate self is not a thing or person, but an *activity*—the activity of recoil and contraction. Aside from that separative activity, there is only the native feeling of wholeness (love)—even while the body-mind-"I" and world continue to arise and change.

What if we didn't practice the habitual gesture of separation? What if (in spite of fear) instead of recoiling from the great current of life, we allowed ourselves to be engulfed in the flow, to participate in it without resistance? Then the sense of separation would vanish. There would be no survival of the independent one who seeks to know and to control. Then we would see that truth is not within, as opposed to without. Truth is ONLY. Truth is Mystery. Our condition is simply free, and we are already whole (complete). Therefore, "within" and "without" are dual aspects of a single, indivisible mystery.

Abiding as the Whole and Fundamental Mystery of consciousness itself, moment to moment, rather than identifying with any of the temporary shapes and configurations that arise as modulations of consciousness, brings the whole body-mind to simple fullness, happiness and peace at its Source— the Heart, the Mystery Itself. Abiding as the Mystery is the same as resting in the luminous current of life, which flows from toe to crown.

Seeking is not required. What is needed instead is an open heart to fully trust and participate in this living mystery play. As Chuang Tzu put it,

"Search for the Tao, and it is nowhere to be found; <u>use</u> the Tao and it is everywhere, inexhaustible."

Emptiness Is Not Empty

"Emptiness" is a troublesome term. Its meaning is too similar to "nothingness" and thus suggests nihilism. Perhaps a more suitable adjective to describe our true nature would be "openness." The mood of existence is that of unlimited openness and capacity (without center or bounds) and absolute wholeness (singularity).

I am uncomfortable with teachers who offhandedly negate body and world. It strikes me as disrespectful to think of the world as an "eclipse" or "disease" or "illusion" imposed upon Original Mind (as some Eastern teachers would have it); or as the lucky "accident" of a "blind watchmaker" (as scientific materialism would have it).

The body, the mind, the world are <u>not</u> a cancer upon God! And they are no accident. Reality Lives! Reality is Alive! Life is the *Way* of Reality; it unfolds in and of Reality. The purpose of life is simply *to be reality*, alive and ever-changing, ever new, ever <u>now</u>.

Therefore, without affirming or negating one atom, see what always, already IS.

Go With the Flow

In human bodily form we naturally feel desires and enjoy the pleasurable and suffer the painful qualities of things, without clinging. We understand that <u>all</u> pleasure, including sexual pleasure, is derived from the Pure Bliss Potential that we always, already Are, and that natural pain is unavoidable.

There is no energy apart from the all-accomplishing Bliss-Potency of the Heart. This Singular Power (envisioned in many cultures as Mother Goddess, and also conceptualized as Radiant Vibration—the Eternal Logos or True Name) comprises every form, pattern, process, quality and event.

This Bright, Dynamic Force forever blazes forth from Primordial Awakeness. Therefore, Freedom (*nirvana*) and Flow (*samsara*) are not two. Freedom Flows. The Heart Shines. We are *Nirvanasara* or Whole Reality.

When we pay careful attention, we readily observe the truth that "All is flow." Because nothing lasts, there are no <u>fixed</u> forms. Therefore, all that appears is self-releasing (automatically liberated).

The Flow cannot be prevented, eliminated, (completely) controlled, avoided, or brought to a halt. No thing or event that appears in the Flow can be retained or repeated. Nothing in the Flow can be made unchanging or absolute. All that appears always disappears. Yet the Heart is never threatened.

All that appears and disappears is spontaneous modulation of the Luminous Signal of the Heart. The miraculous and infinitely complex display of patterns and processes—worlds within worlds within worlds—streams on and on in vast circles of life, without beginning or end.

> As it was in the beginning
> Is now, and ever shall be:
> Worlds without end.
> Amen, Amen.
> (common prayer in Anglican Church)

> The Tao is never-ending;
> Being never-ending, it is far-reaching;
> Being far-reaching, it is returning;
> Returning to source, it is never-ending.
> (Lao Tzu)

We are the streaming waves of the Clear Light Ocean. Any experience, however pleasurable or painful, is a temporary play upon this Heart of Pure Capacity. When radically intuited, the Perfect Capacity reveals itself as Mystery-Radiance, or Free Love-Bliss.

The Heart radically knows itself as the Basis of all. No matter where it looks, it discovers no thing independent from its own Self-Existing Bliss. Every form, pattern, process, quality and event rise and fall within its Flow.

However, from the distorted view of a separately existing self, all that appears is "other." Thus, all that arises—even pleasurable experiences—appear as confrontation.

In its quest for survival, the ego-self chronically recoils, withdrawing from everything and everyone in order to survive in isolation (safety) from all that arises. Therefore, the separate self feels fear (and is fear). Fear *is* the separative gesture, the recoil, the contraction. That is it, precisely.

The separate one craves security to the degree that it is unwilling to be born. Those beings who have not yet awakened beyond the illusion of separate self are always withholding from life—they are not fully born, completely present and alive.

From the view of the independent ego, the Spirit-Current of Life (to the degree that it is felt at all) *is experienced as the very current of danger and death*, the destroyer of the separate self! It is Energy and Life and Irreversible Flow, not stasis and solidity and the survival of separate forms. Therefore, the separative ego resists and rejects the Current of Life! (In theological terms, the soul rejects and denies the Holy Spirit of God.)

In truth, the Current of Life *is* the destroyer of the separate self! But such "destruction" (de-structuring) is liberation and salvation into Real Life, Divine Life. Life is self-releasing, always surrendered into its own resurrecting (or ever-new and ever-alive) Current. All of cosmos is sacrificial worship of the eternally living, bright source.

May all beings relax into the Current of Life, which destroys only what is limited and false. (How can it destroy what is uncaused and Real?) May all beings fall into the Heart and be lived by God, the mystery and power of consciousness itself.

Evil Is Not an Entity, But an Error

Evil is not an *entity*. "Satan" (as a being, person or entity) simply does not exist.

Evil is not a power; not an independently existing (self-abiding) negative force.

Nor is evil any kind of *thing* (any particular object), in itself.

Just as cancer is not other than the body's own cells in a diseased state, evil is the human heart in a state of ignorance and dis-ease. Evil can be further defined or characterized as the refusal of relationship—withdrawing from life through the heart's recoil from family and friends and local and world community. Evil is the activity of isolating, and *thus* fearing, and *thus* hating. Evil begins when love, empathy, compassion and relationship fail. Evil begins with making people and things into the "other."

Likewise, hell is not a place or realm. Like evil, it is a condition of one's own heart. Hell is refusal of relationship, or primal love.

When everyone is seen as oneself, evil does not reign, war does not erupt, greed does not corrupt, hell is unmade and peace (or heaven) is possible.

The Way of Wholeness

"Whatever we resist tends to persist." Carl Jung

Whole awareness[27] is the only "control" of life and experience. All else is attack or retreat from a split-off (imaginary) position. Fighting or fleeing any unwanted experience *does not help to set you free of suffering.*

Fighting produces tension, anger, hatred and frustration; and the sense of endless combat against an enemy who cannot be destroyed. Fleeing dramatizes fear, shame and despair; and the sense of being chased or stalked by an enemy who cannot be escaped.

Whether fighting or fleeing, such avoidance behavior is a vicious circle: it produces more of the pain that you struggle to erase or escape. Until the advent of continuous whole awareness, there is no graduation from the school of suffering.

To become free of suffering, you must live as wholeness (radical non-avoidance, non-separation). The word "whole" shares its

---

[27] "Whole awareness" is my term for what Buddhists call "mindfulness." I have chosen the different label because "mindfulness" actually involves the whole body's emotional intelligence (beyond what most people think of as "the mind") thus the term can be misleading.

etymological root and meaning with the words
"hale" and "health" and "well." Well-being is whole
being.

The Way of Wholeness is the moment to
moment practice of wholeness. It is to NOW look
and act and feel and be whole.

But what if you're feeling painful anxiety or
jealousy, anger or sorrow? Your practice of
wholeness must pass the "test" of your own pain
(that is, you must allow yourself to FEEL your own
pain).

Be whole with your feelings. Feel them with
full awareness. And through wholly *feeling* your body-
mind contraction, *feel through* and beyond the
contraction, to Wholeness.

Practice wholeness. It is the truly intelligent
relationship with yourself, the non-reactive embrace
and understanding of your own suffering. Such a
way is without dilemma, while the reactive approach
to afflictive emotions is strife (and keeps the ego
bound to a self-propagating loop of self-fear, self-
war and self-hate).

This affirmation may help:

Wholeness is truth and whole
awareness operates in truth. Whole
awareness is the intelligence of the
Whole Condition—not a separate,
limited, false position (the self-image).
Therefore, with loving kindness, I
intend to practice the Way of
Wholeness.

When anguish arises, I won't try to
escape it or make it vanish. I will allow
it to be exactly what it is. Indeed, I will
open to the pain—lean *into* it with
relaxed mind and soft belly. Through

wholeness, may I clearly understand my own suffering.

In wholeness (radical non-avoidance, non-duality) "I" (the whole body-mind) am responsible—able to respond appropriately to whatever arises. May I always live as Whole Awareness, and may the fruits of this practice of Whole Awareness benefit all beings.

Carl Jung on the Pitfall of Ego-Inflation

In the Zen tradition, one who becomes enlightened is obligated to wait *at least* six years before beginning to teach; this is to allow time for the "stink of enlightenment" to wear off. Such an irreverent and humorous take on enlightened life—beautifully expressed in Chan, Zen, and some Sufi and Hasidic wisdom tales—is a powerful preventative medicine against the mental illness of ego-inflation.

Ego-inflation is a potential pitfall—Jung would call it a "shadow"—for anyone practicing a "spiritual path." Indeed, without the prerequisite humor, honesty and humility, the danger only increases as one's practice advances into the "higher" stages.

In its mild and most common form, ego-inflation shows up as holier-than-thou attitudes and the mentality that "My way is the *only* way." Of course, this degree of ego-inflation is not usually madness, but simple ignorance and naiveté, but displayed as arrogance. By contrast, the severest form of ego-inflation is actual psychosis: a runaway messianic complex that convinces you that you are a "perfect" embodiment of something "special," called upon to deliver a "unique" gift that was unavailable to humanity before your "miraculous" birth. Your

140

rants begin to sound like ad copy, studded with superlatives about your glories: *never-before-seen, exclusive offer, elite company, the best, the highest, the first, the last, the only,* etc.

Carl Jung discusses ego-inflation (more often just called "inflation") in Volume XI of *The Collected Works, Two Essays on Analytical Psychology.* In Chapter IV, *Negative Attempts to Free the Individuality,* he writes:

> Probably no one who was conscious of the absurdity of this identification would have the courage to make a principle of it. But the danger is that very many people lack the necessary humor, or else it fails them at this particular juncture: they are seized by a sort of pathos, everything seems pregnant with meaning, and *all effective self-criticism is checked.*

Aside from imagining oneself a prophet, ego also can be seduced by a related form of inflation: the dizzying rush of identifying with a person or path that claims that he or it is the Perfect Way.

> There is another alluring joy, subtler and apparently more legitimate: the joy of becoming a prophet's disciple. This, for the vast majority of people, is an altogether ideal technique. Its advantages are: the *odium dignitatis,* the superhuman responsibility of the prophet, turns into the so much sweeter *odium indignatis.* The disciple is unworthy; modestly he sits at the Master's feet and guards against having ideas of his own.

Mental laziness becomes a virtue;
one can at least bask in the sun of
a semi-divine being. He can enjoy
the archaism and infantilism of his
unconscious fantasies without loss
to himself, for all responsibility is
laid at the Master's door. Through
his deification of the Master, the
disciple, apparently without
noticing it, waxes in stature;
moreover, does he not possess the
great truth—not from his own
discovery, of course, but received
straight from the Master's hands?
Naturally the disciples always stick
together, not out of love, but for
the very understandable purpose
of effortlessly confirming their
own convictions by engendering
an air of collective agreement.

As Jung drily notes, "The gratifications of
the accompanying inflation at least do something to
make up for the loss of spiritual freedom."

He ends his essay with a powerful warning:
"All this is so humanly understandable that it would
be a matter for astonishment if it led to any further
destination whatever."

Every "I" is Life's Process

"I" is not an object, not a fixed and concrete self, not an independent entity.

"I" is a *process*. The process that is "I" inextricably belongs to the universal process, the cosmic life, the Great Way.

To dislike yourself is not to dislike a static and permanent entity (*There is no such one!*) but to dislike what is actually a *process* of awakening. And such contracted feeling is a hindrance to that very awakening.

To love yourself is not to be in love with and identified with a solid, independent entity, but to love, respect, support and trust the life *process* that is "I". To love the evolutionary process, the mind-stream that is "I", is to be in accord with the Great Way of awakening and happiness.

Therefore, today, love yourself. Have faith in the Great Way and its process, called "I".

Love yourself wholly. Be happy. Happiness is your first responsibility and your first form of service to all others.

THIS Is As God As It Gets

"Suffering is its own cure." (Rumi)

All seeking becomes, at last, obsolete. But when? *When* does the career of seeking come to an end? When will the war, the struggle, be over for <u>you</u>?

When will you acknowledge that you do not know what a single thing *IS*?

When will you stop clinging to form because you understand that form is completely empty?

When will you stop trying to shed form because you understand that emptiness <u>IS</u> form? (And thus you are free to "Let go of letting go.")

In other words, when will you abandon the *principle* of all your concerns and all your strategies (the terrifying principle of the isolated, limited self, split apart from the Life-Source and exiled from the heart)?

How long are you willing to suffer, to presume your independence from God (Reality, Identity) and therefore to seek and seek and seek God?

Seeking is an exercise in dilemma! To seek God is to presume separation and then to *practice* separation. Seeking is rehearsing suffering, rather than practicing happiness by relaxing, now and now, into Lucid Presence.

I cannot grasp for what I AM. My only prayer is "Amen"—"So BE it."

I AM the Heart, not by virtue of a flawless ego, not because of pure thoughts, perfect discipline, good works, accumulated merit, or a tamed mind. Not because of anything. I simply am the Heart already, prior to everything, and inclusive of everything.

All those who abide as the Heart can only BE what they always, already ARE. This is not a choice. There is no alternative. It is Reality.

I am the Self who never rejects a single quantum of any world.

I am the Self who always includes every form in every world.

Therefore, Self _is_ form. Form _is_ Self. The Heart and its Light are One.

If you do not understand this, words cannot further explain it.

All the World's a Stage.

The whole shebang is a spontaneous display of conscious energy. And at the end of this divine theater, where does it go? The conscious energy remains after the play has gone. Then a new act, a new cosmos, begins. Meanwhile, enjoy your role in the drama and in THIS moment and play your part BIG—to the back of the house!

> From William Shakespeare's *A Midsummer Night's Dream:*
>
> Be cheerful, sir:
> Our revels now are ended. These our actors,
> as I foretold you,
> Were all spirits and are melted into air, into thin air:
> And, like the baseless fabric of this vision,
> The cloud-capped towers, the gorgeous palaces,
> The solemn temples, the great globe itself,
> Yea, all which it inherit, shall dissolve.
> And, like this insubstantial pageant faded,
> Leave not a rack behind.
> We are such stuff as dreams are made on,
> And our little life is rounded with a sleep.

What he said!

Or as they say in Buddhism: "All *dharmas* are empty." ("Dharmas" can be translated as "paths" or "processes.") The entire phenomenal world is only Flow. Everything that comes and goes is no more substantial (ultimately) than a dream. Its basis is empty, unknowable, ungraspable and irreducible. Like events in a dream, all the worlds arise and fall without permanent meaning, implication, or effect. This "emptiness" is beyond comparison or correlation. It is traceless—beyond all information.

Everyone has his or her own unique path, *but there is no alternative to emptiness.* Emptiness is the nature of everyone, everything, whatever the path. Emptiness is at the heart of you, me, and everyone. All dharmas are empty. That is their condition.

(Now read the above two paragraphs replacing the words "empty" and "emptiness" with "space." Try it with "openness.")

Everything Is Everything

The Buddhist teaching of "mutually dependent arising" states that anything that appears is interdependent with everything else; there is no isolatable, independently abiding or arising thing or event.

William Carlos Williams wrote a great little poem that reveals the kernel:

So much depends
Upon

a red wheel
barrow

glazed with rain
water

beside the white
chickens.

PART FIVE

Sexual Communion

ADYASHAKTI

Moisture

There are two sides to the coin of enlightenment; two inseparable halves that form a whole. Traditionally, in Mahayana Buddhism, these two aspects were labeled *wisdom* and *compassion*. I prefer to call these twins, *freedom* and *love*. Without the realization and development of both these fundamental and complimentary principles—freedom and love—one cannot be completely awake or completely happy.

The practice of deep meditation soon makes obvious the emptiness of all phenomena, and an aura of freedom appears. When this intuition of original, free being waxes potent enough, dependencies and addictions may shrivel and fall like dead leaves. (Or not. Alan Watts and Chogyam Trungpa—eloquent teachers of the enlightened view—were both winos; Nisargatta Maharaj, a modern Advaitin, chain smoked.) But even those who have tasted this *satori*—this essential freedom from the "stuff" of life—will remain incomplete personalities, unless they also exercise and develop the complimentary agency of loving relationships.

Too often, I have seen students (particularly from the more intellectual, less devotional, traditions, such as Zen and Advaita Vedanta) stuck in what the sages of old called "void sickness"—tending in their characters toward dissociation, indifference, fatalism, dryness. The main reason most outsiders misunderstand Zen as nihilism is because so many Zen Buddhists are nihilists! These abstract, arid, in-their-head-types (male and female), who populate every Zen and Advaita school, East and West, direly need the refreshment of a good, sweet, moist communion with the living Earth. (You know exactly what I mean!) The communication of non-dual wisdom for modern times must include a generous splash of Eros, laughter and love.

Life Is Erotic At Origin

- *Adyashakti* (Primordial Energy[28]) is the origin and creative basis of all cosmic and human evolution and all life functions, altogether.

- The human body emerges from Whole Life like a plum emerges from a plum tree. Every human being is the embodiment of the creative power: We are models of the macrocosm; the incarnation of Mystery-Radiance.

- Sexual desire, pleasure and orgasm arise as functions of Whole Life Energy. Therefore, our sexuality belongs to Whole Life, exists in Whole Life, and does not appear except in and of Whole Life. Every other function also belongs to the same all-comprising, all-accomplishing, evolutionary power. *There is no other power.*

---

[28] Called *Shakti* or *Kundalini* in Hindu and Buddhist Tantra, *chi* in Taoism, and *elan vital, holy spirit*, etc., in Western schools of mysticism.

- <u>All</u> creative power is here and now, at the Heart.

- Sexual experience is a stepped-down modulation of the Absolute Intensity of Whole Life Energy at Infinity.

- The fulfillment of human life (and human sexuality) is in the awakening of consciousness and the conductivity of primordial power. It is a matter of completely (without resistance or blockage or self-holding) *embodying* the freedom of the Heart and the radiance of life.

- Any person who embodies the divine creative power (even those who choose to be celibate) realizes the union of Consciousness and Radiance—and his or her enjoyment and emotional fulfillment is ongoing and complete.

- Whole Life Energy Itself is sexually active as us and through us, bodily. Even more fundamentally, Whole Life Energy Itself is "sexually" active as the Primordial Creative Evolutionary Power. From electromagnetic forces, to atoms and molecules, to plants and animals and humans, to metaphorical gods and goddesses, Whole Life Energy Itself continuously displays its inherent "sexuality" (the polarized dynamic interaction of Conscious Energy).

- We cannot compare our own unique personalities to the personalities of others. All of us are unduplicated variations of Real

Being. Therefore, we cannot compare our own unique sexuality to the sexuality of others. All sexuality appears within the Only One, but all of us are unique <u>variations</u> of this Real (and Total) Personality.

- We can always enjoy emotional-energy pleasure, just by feeling and breathing and smiling. Such pleasure is related to erotic pleasure (breathing is a basic and joyous exchange of life-energy).

- Those who are awake to the energy body are able to participate consciously in the continuous flow and exchange of Life-Force. Such energy-communion is a subtle sensual pleasure that is available during interludes of repose, meditation, lovemaking and also at random moments throughout the day. In other words, even when we are not physically making love, we can abide <u>in</u> love—now—in the embrace of Life, and that embrace is not neutral and static, but charged with the delicious flow of polarized life-force.

Cosmo-Erotic Metaphors

How does one write intelligibly about what is beyond
words? All metaphors are a pain in the ass (not an
actual ache in the *gluteus maximus*—I'm speaking
metaphorically), because words are clumsy,
reductionist fragments of whole experience.

Once, while sunk deep in meditation, I felt
myself merge with a central column of thundering,
bright energy that stood buzzing and erect in my
body and then shot upward like a violent geyser of
lightning, piercing the core of an indescribably
gorgeous, self-luminous white flower that spread its
petals above the crown of my head. At the moment
of penetration or union, I felt myself to be the
infinite presence of radiant power that pervades
every atom of the cosmos.

Were those metaphors sexual enough?

The experience itself was orgasmic, indeed
beyond any sexual orgasm I have ever known.
Nevertheless, describing it verbally stumbles into the
problem of gendered language. When I wrote about
the experience, using the traditional metaphors of
Shakti merging with Shiva, a feminist friend of mine
took offense. "Is reality male and female?" she
demanded. "Does reality have gender?"

Well…no, of course not…and…yes, sort of.
Not *gender* gender. There are no genitalia involved.

Oh, but the polarized dynamic of <u>energy</u>! My
Goddess! The world is every day doing things with
thunderclouds, oceans and stars that human lovers
are not bold enough to try. This Shakti—Eros—
energy exchange—is the powerhouse behind the birth
and evolution and death of the cosmos. Let us not
pretend it doesn't have the power to tweak our
emotions just a little.

As to the kundalini incident described
above, it was "erotic" in the most complete sense of
the word, but it was entirely non-genital: it took
place within the subtle body. Perhaps the kundalini
experience would be different—lacking the
masculine orientation—when such energy arousal is
enjoyed by a female meditator.

Metaphors and pronouns! He, She, It, You,
Me, We, Us. None of them <u>absolutely </u>real.
Nonetheless, they seem a useful way of describing
subjective experience.

In Jewish, Christian and Islamic "bridal
mysticism," every soul—of man or woman—is
regarded as <u>female</u>, the vessel or "Holy Grail" of the
all-pervading (all-penetrating) power of the Holy
Spirit. St. Teresa of Avila called herself a "bride of
Christ." She experienced the movement of life-force
as an overwhelmingly powerful erotic awakening and
opening of her total body-mind. "Christ's spirit
pierced my heart like an arrow," Teresa wrote. She
said it permeated her whole body and drew her up
into the Godhead, into a perfect embrace in which
she disappeared in unity.

Hindu Tantrism provides the
metaphor/model of Shiva-Shakti: "He"
(Consciousness <u>itself</u>) is in union with "Her" (radiant
energy and matter). Much of Hindu Tantric
iconography is <u>explicitly</u> sexual (penises penetrating
vaginas, oh my!).

Yet Buddhist Tantra gives the reverse of the Hindu Tantric picture (further illustrating that such models are only metaphors). In Tibetan Buddhism, the radiant, active spirit is "male" and represents *upaya* (skillful means, the all-accomplishing power), and *karuna* (compassion)—while the absolute nature is regarded as "female" and represents *shunyata* (emptiness) and *prajna* (wisdom, insight into emptiness). The integration and equation of Emptiness and Form (or Freedom and Love) completes the stages of enlightenment in these schools.

Then again, in Shaktism, where devotees worship Ma Shakti as Divine Mother, "She" (primordial creative energy) merges with "Herself" as *Parashakti* (Void, beyond the manifest dimensions). In other words, it is all the Divine Mother. (Deep-rooted feminists, apply here.)

However one reduces it to words, one thing seems clear to me: This dynamo of yin-yang, yab-yum, "male"-"female" *drives the whole material creation.* It says in the *Tao Teh Ching*, "In the beginning was the Tao, and the Tao became One, and the One became Two, and the Two became ten-thousand things." From my own meditative experience, it appears that these "Two"—the primal polarity or primordial couple—persist all the way "up" through the "higher" dimensions—right up until "merging with the Beloved." So these male-female sexual metaphors, while certainly not absolutely real, express something close to the heart of life. An Upanishad says, "Desire creates the universe, sustains it and dissolves it." For this reason, I deeply appreciate the honesty and wisdom of the sexual iconography of Tantra. Many other spiritual paths seem to ignore or fear the erotic aspect of the journey of becoming whole. Of course the icons of Buddhas in sexual union are not merely sexual—but they are also not less than sexual. Their sexuality is obvious and indelible, not hidden or neglected. Yes, their sexual energy is a subset of their spiritual energy; yet it is never denied, but simply transcended.

On the surface, there appears to be a contradiction between Shakti-based traditions (Tantric yoga, Kundalini yoga, Kashmir Shaivism, Siddha yoga, Sri Aurobindo's Integral Yoga, etc.) and the radically intuitive teachings of Self-realization (Zen, Dzogchen, Advaita Vedanta, etc.).

The Shakti practices rely on devotional surrender, the initiatory grace of the guru and/or Goddess (directly), and the dynamic workings of kundalini. These approaches appear to be evolutionary (progressive) paths of ascent (or return) to ever higher and more inclusive levels of consciousness and power.

By contrast, the Self-realization practices rely on the sword of wisdom that cuts through the illusion of limited identity to reveal one's Original Face. These can often be characterized as "sudden" enlightenment schools—not evolutionary, but revolutionary; not vertical and hierarchical, but "horizontal" and absolute. Not a matter of ascent or return to the source, but a matter of the radical transcendence of all dualities, including "low" and "high," "world" and "source."

I believe, however, that these twin approaches differ mostly in emphasis, not in ultimate realization. In actual practice, the experiences and effects of these two paths overlap and interact synergistically. When Shakti surges through the body-mind, it awakens profound insights and releases tremendous energy that may lead consciousness (in the most profound cases) to union with Shiva (the absolute Self). Therefore, the event of Shakti arousal can lead to moments of perfect, non-dual awareness.

From the other emphasis, when one deeply intuits the limitless, non-dual nature (Shiva) behind all appearances, Kundalini (Shakti) often is spontaneously aroused. This is the sequence of events in my own case. Indeed, from what I have read and heard from other practitioners, Kundalini experiences are likely during the higher stages of <u>any</u> meditation practice (even such "empty" and non-devotional approaches as Zen).

Ramana Maharshi would explain that we exist at all levels at the same time, because we are simply Whole. We <u>are</u> Shiva-Shakti, not in part, but entirely. On the absolute level, we intuit the Heart (Shiva), the clear-light space in which everything appears. On the relative level, we experience Shakti rejuvenating and transforming the manifest personality and world.

A number of mystical traditions label these complementary poles of the divine dynamo, "male" and "female" (most often, a male Holy Spirit/Intelligence or its analog and a female Soul or its analog). Perhaps we could invent better metaphors, genderless terms. My feminist friend is correct that "male" and "female" are not absolute categories, not ontological realities.

However, those who personally engage the interplay of conscious energy and matter in their own bodies will smile with recognition when they encounter models for this spiritual process that relate it to the sexual embrace of woman and man. Yes, it is like that, only much more *fundamental*. This polarity at the root of being is the profound basis of sexual love. Ask Teresa of Avila, the Bride of Christ—or better still, find out for yourself.

A Summary of the Process of Awakening

The journey of awakening can be summed in one line: Love Whole Life until you awaken as Whole Life.

Want more detail? I once read of a Buddhist Tantra that categorizes the path of awakening in four stages: Seeking, Meeting, Embracing, and Orgasm. I liked the metaphor, so I've expanded upon it here:

I.   BEGINNING STAGE: *SEEKING*
        Find a path with heart.

II.   SECOND STAGE: *MEETING*
        In the earliest stage of awakening, the Heart is encountered as Presence, and its Radiance is felt as a Current of Energy circulating (ascending and descending) in the body-mind. The appropriate practice at this early stage is love, devotion and surrender in communion with the Presence and its Bright Power. Such divine remembrance may be aided by singing, chanting, prayer, dance, *mantra*[29], prayer-of-the-heart[30] (and, in

---

[29] The inner repetition during formal meditation (and also at random during the day), of an empowering phrase, such as,

general, creating sacred space and occasion). Meditation at this beginning stage makes use of prayer, mantra or simply following the in-and-out sweep of the breath.

During this beginner's stage, one works with the Buddhist Precepts, the Boddhisattva vows (See: Buddha's Greatest Hits later in this volume) and the practice of loving-kindness ("May I be loving and kind. May all beings be loving and kind.")

As a consequence of these practices, the Life Energy may be suddenly aroused and released and felt to powerfully rise or descend in the body-mind; this is the Grace of Spirit-Baptism. The practice in such moments is to deeply relax and go with the flow of the Life-Force, which produces healing, opening and quickening effects.[31]

III. THIRD STAGE: *EMBRACING*

In the next stage of practice, one spends more time sitting in meditation, up to (but not more than) two hours a day (divided into a morning and an evening session). The meditator moves beyond the

---

"Om Ma." The mantra is joined to one's breathing (out-breath: "Om," in-breath: "Ma").

[30] A prayer spoken silently and inwardly, at the heart-center, as a continuous invocation. A well-known example from early Christianity is the Jesus Prayer (also called Prayer of the Heart): "Jesus Christ, Savior, have mercy on my heart." You can compose your own invocation, or try: "Giver of Life, thank you."

[31] This release of latent Life Energy in some cases quickly takes awareness all the way to the third stage and "Orgasm"—that is, merging in the infinite Clear Light.

technique of mantra and following the breath, and develops silent meditation: watching thought-forms and sensations come and go while continually recognizing their fundamental emptiness. This stage of deepening silence may be aided by various traditional inquiries, such as:

- "What *is* it?" (Also, "Where *is* it?")
- "Who (or What) is aware of this?"
- "Who (or What) am 'I'?"

IV. FOURTH STAGE: *ORGASM*

In this stage of awakening, one moves into profoundly deep meditation, which culminates in Divine Union (which could appropriately be called Divine Orgasm). That is, one literally merges with the Heart and its Radiance. This is the experience of mystical absorption in the Infinite Brightness, or Clear Light of Void,[32] marked by (temporary) ego-dissolution and unspeakable bliss.

Although this event of merging in the Godhead is valued by some yogic paths as the highest degree of self-realization, it is actually an exclusive (and therefore, incomplete) awakening, because it occurs only during the utter forgetting of body-mind and world.[33] Clinging to this inner bliss is known in Zen as "void sickness."[34]

---

[32] There is an ancient Buddhist mantra, "Gone, gone, gone beyond; Gone beyond the beyond; Fully awake, so be it!" This transcendent experience is expressed by the middle phrase, "Gone beyond."

[33] This mystical union is called, in Sanskrit, *nirvikalpa samadhi*, meaning "absorption in formlessness." One falls

V. COMPLETION STAGE: *INTEGRATION*

The final (and ongoing) stage of awakening is Integration, or maturing in Love, in which one abides as the Heart (Freedom-Peace-Emptiness) and its Light (Love-Bliss-Energy), while actively embracing Life (or the total world-body-mind). There is no formal practice at this completion stage of enlightenment. Rather, one's integrated actions will have become very simple, direct, spontaneous and full. Ramana Maharshi called this stage *sahaja*, meaning *effortless.*[35] The awakened Heart naturally abides as the Absolute Subject, the unity of the Light (above) and the Life (below).

COMMENTARY:

The stages of awakening leading to Integration do not necessarily proceed in the order

---

into the Heart in a deep inward trance, oblivious to body, mind and world.

[34] It seems possible to me that the event of merging in the Original Light is not absolutely necessary to full awakening. Blissful though it is, I do not seek to return to the Light. More to the point, freedom does not depend on such experience. On the other hand, every high-level adept I've ever encountered has had this experience. It may be that the experience is needless, yet *inevitable* at a certain stage of meditation.

[35] In the Buddhist mantra mentioned in the fourth footnote, this integration (rebirth) into fully human/divine life is expressed by the phrase, "Gone *beyond* the beyond." In other words, gone full circle. "Fully awake, so be it!"

mentioned. (For example, a person might "begin" the whole affair with an intense Clear Light experience, as happened in my case.) Some persons awaken to the freedom of their own nature in a relatively short time—or, in rare cases, instantly.[36] Yet it is necessary to the full process of Integration that the abilities learned at each "progressive" stage be cultivated. For example, the passion of devotion, and the tenderness of loving-kindness (first stage), and the ease of recognizing one's own mind-forms as self-made illusion (second stage), are crucial capacities. These skills may come to a person spontaneously, or with little effort. But whatever the case, these faculties are indispensable to living an integrated, enlightened life.[37]

Zen Buddhism considers awakening the "middle" stage of the path, the comparatively easy part. Developing the integrity to live *as* the Heart is the lifetime journey. Also, spiritual awakening occurs at varying degrees of depth; only in rare cases is it incontrovertible. For most persons, after awakening to the limitless view, there is a rapid or gradual return to identifying with limits, and the need for further practice (devotional surrender, loving-kindness, meditation, etc.). It is important to understand that the phenomenal world does not go

---

[36] Ramana Maharshi spontaneously awakened at age 16, during an episode in which he was suddenly overcome by the fear of dying. Instead of fleeing his panic, he lay down and imagined the entire death process, dropping layers of identity, until he finally realized that he was the deathless reality that supports it all.

[37] In addition to such indispensable skills, various spiritual gifts (such as clairvoyance) sometimes develop spontaneously. It must be understood that these powers have nothing to do with awakeness directly. They are, at best, secondary to awakeness, and more often, simply irrelevant (like being left-handed).

away. Rather, one lives from a new view and relationship to body and mind and all changes. This enlightened view is that of inherent freedom and wholeness, bodily relaxed in the flow, rather than contracted identification with any parts or functions as if they existed independently of Total Life.

Awakening from the dream of limited identity occurs outside the dream, outside of time. Our original condition, upstream from the dream, *IS* only awakeness. Therefore, our "enlightenment" is most prior, tacit, implicit and already perfectly complete. And this awakening cannot be the result of individual effort. That is, it is not caused by any or all of our seeking, pushing, pulling, trying, struggling, warring, clinging, avoiding, or knowing. It is what we are, not anything that we can become.

Thus, you deeply awaken to and as the Great Process itself, not because of superior virtue or any *specialness*. You awaken without cause. Awakeness IS reality, entirely uncaused (and therefore, not dependent on anything at all). You clearly intuit your true condition, and it is freedom.

The awakened mind admits of no levels or partial values within its Wholeness. Just as there are no degrees of pregnancy ("Mom, I'm sort of pregnant."), there are no degrees of reality. *Reality is only indivisibly total.*

However, there are different degrees of *stabilization* of this awakening, and of the freedom and peace that accompany it. Some people wake up so fully (i.e., are so stable in their understanding) that they remain in a more or less transfigured condition once and for all (the Indian sage, Ramana Maharshi, comes to mind). But most of us fall into and out of the Heart of Wholeness; drawn back to separative identification with various phenomena in themselves. Very few awakenings are so stable that there are no further complications in relation to money, food and sex; the vital-life areas that cause most ego-entanglements.

Therefore, in most cases, moments of profoundly enlightened awareness and bliss come and go again and again; meanwhile the <u>ongoing</u> work is *integration* or *personalization* of the awakened heart-mind in daily life.

As the American Buddhist teacher Jack Kornfield puts it, "After the ecstasy, the laundry."

"Spirit versus Flesh" Is an Ancient Falsehood

The imagined dichotomy between Spirit and flesh (or emptiness and form) is radically false. No such split has occurred or will occur. Existence is never dual.

1. Fundamentally, there is no dilemma. No split, no gap, no division. The war between Spirit and flesh must be utterly abandoned.

2. One need not choose between Spirit *and* flesh; indeed, no such alternative is possible! Spirit is Reality, and flesh (or all form) is the <u>function</u> of Reality. The first cannot be attained; the latter cannot be avoided or rejected.

3. Try and try and try to rise above the body and all forms and functions. All such striving shall be only dilemma, and in vain.

4. Ascetic strivers who seek to escape upwards out of the body (into the subtle realms above) seek to achieve the impossible. No matter how abstracted one becomes, one is

still compelled to breathe, drink, eat, urinate and defecate, to sleep and dream.

5.   The body and its changes (and <u>all</u> phenomena and <u>all</u> changes) can never be escaped.

6.   *Understand*: There is no escape. Now cease altogether your struggles to escape!

ADYASHAKTI

PART SIX

Go Gentle into That Goodnight

ADYASHAKTI

Death Is Real

The ego-"I" is temporary. In deep surrender, "I" dissolves. But trust that the dissolution of ego is NOT annihilation; not when it occurs in dreamless sleep or in dreamless awakeness, nor in drug-induced ecstasy, nor at the advent of deep orgasm, nor when the ego melts with bodily death at the end of a lifetime. Never is ego-dissolution annihilation.

Death is real, if by "death" we mean endless change or perfect sacrifice, the passing away of every arising form, from physical to subtle, without any exceptions whatsoever. But there is no such thing as death if by "death" we mean annihilation. The uncreated and indestructible Person cannot even be diminished, let alone eliminated.

When Ramana Maharshi was fading fast from cancer, his devotees wept and begged him not to leave them. He laughed. "Where can I go?" he said. "I am Here."

When Free Radiant Intelligence identifies itself with the body-mind "I" and its changes, not realizing its own supreme condition, it is like someone dreaming of a unicorn and believing himself to be that unicorn. Upon waking, it is clear that the unicorn was merely a form arising within the dreaming mind. The mind is not the unicorn, nor is it any other figment within the dream. The identity of the unicorn is in its source, the mind, which, while being the basis of the unicorn's spontaneous appearance, is quite beyond "unicorn-ness".

Similarly, "I" is merely a function appearing and disappearing within Timeless Intelligence, along with all other functions as a whole system. The Timeless One, as the Identity of "I" (and everything not-"I"), freely permits "I" (and everything not-"I") to appear and disappear. No clinging, no recoiling. When manifest conditions grow karmically ripe, the Intelligence spontaneously awakens and realizes its actual transcendental nature and unqualified condition. Such enlightenment is ordinary, not crazy or spectacular.

In Dzogchen, enlightened mind is called "Great Natural Perfection." Natural, as in "native" and "ordinary"—not special or exceptional. In fact, enlightenment is very much down to earth. It feels grounded. A Greek mystic, Heraclitus, said, "The way up is the same as the way down."

Whatever I can say to you will always distill to this core message: Trust in your own Source; it is Benevolent. It is okay to let go. It is okay to die. It is okay.

Shadows Sweep the Stairs but Raise No Dust

"I hold your quickly fading photograph in my more slowly fading hand." (Ranier Maria Rilke)

"He not busy being born is busy dying." (Bob Dylan)

I have orbited the sun more than 60 times, and I have something to report: Solomon was mistaken. Solomon the Wise, son of David, King of Israel, preacher of Ecclesiastes, misspoke. Not when he said, "Vanity of vanities, all is vanity." He sure got that right! But he didn't deconstruct our situation far enough. He still claimed, "The Earth abides forever, the sun also rises." (Sound of buzzer.) I'm sorry but that answer is incorrect.

It's not just you and I who are vulnerable and mortal. The Earth does not abide forever, the sun also dies. In about 6 billion years, the sun will deplete its hydrogen fuel and flare into a red giant, charring the earth into a cinder.

Nothing lasts. Even the sun—the very sun, itself!—follows the same trajectory as a mayfly. Here today, gone tomorrow. You, me, our loved ones, our enemies, our children and grandchildren—we all are as temporary as snowmen. Where are the snowmen of yesteryear?

Everything, from quarks to quasars, is merely mortal, an appearance, a fleeting pattern, an eddy in a stream, a sumo wrestler in a cloud changing into a ballerina, then—*Poof!*

Death is no stranger, stalking us from a distance until it attacks. Death is an inherent function within the unbroken and unbreakable process that we are. Death is not the opposite and opponent of life. Life IS birth-death. The same process that gave us birth grants us death—and we ARE that process. We've just been thinking of the whole progression by half of its reality.

BUT CONSIDER THIS:

The endless stream of countless deaths has not altered the fragility of flowers. Orchids are still softer than silk. Newborns emerge from their mother's wombs equipped with no more armor than Adam wore when Lucy gave him birth in Africa. This suggests an untouchable condition here at play, an uncreated and indestructible nature that moves through the process of birth and change and death like John Coltrane gliding through the scales on "Favorite Things."

No Escape

My father clung to his dying body like a shipwrecked sailor on a deflating raft. He had bladder, stomach and lung cancer, kidney failure, Parkinson's disease and heart disease—yet he requested in writing to be revived by all means if he slipped into a coma! As it happened, a team of mechanics used their plungers, bicycle pumps and cattle prods but never brought him out of his coma.

Each of us will see how it goes when it's our turn to drop dead. None of us has a smoke ring's chance in a whirlwind of survival as an independent, encapsulated, private self. But maybe there is something wrong with that model of the self. Maybe it's not an accurate description of our condition.

When a student asked the Buddha if there was a self that survived death, the Buddha answered, "When a fire is extinguished, in which direction does it go—north, south, east or west?"

Meditation practice, from a certain view, is training in conscious dying. It prepares the body-mind to relax and ease into the unknown without resistance and panic. Likewise, contemplating the truth of "no escape" helps us to utterly abandon the search for escape.

This reminds me of a bumper sticker: "Life is a lot easier now that I've given up all hope." Most would label this nihilism. But I feel peace when I rest in my own nature, honestly, which means in innocence of all religious beliefs, baring my heart unto What IS.

It's dumbfounding.

It's liberating.

Student: "What is the meaning of Zen?"

Teacher: "If Zen has any special meaning, I myself am not enlightened."

Surrender All the Way through Ego-"Death"

Ego-"I" is a *function*, and like all functions, it comes and goes spontaneously. When you fall asleep at night you begin by dreaming, in which some version of ego still operates (projected from the deep psyche), but gradually you slip into dreamless sleep, in which there is absolutely no "I" (no apparent ego-entity) arising.

Tens of thousands of times, you have passed into dreamless sleep. That is to say, the ego-function has ceased entirely, coming to rest at its root. And tens of thousands of times, you have passed through dreams and then reawakened to awareness of the physical world. Therefore, you have already gone through ego "death" many times! It is no big deal to submerge into deep sleep, right? In the morning, spontaneously, ego-"I" re-emerges.

Consider this: "I" does not wake *itself* up every morning. From the root into which "I" has dissolved in deep sleep, "I" is once again awakened (re-generated). The wonderful Being responsible for bodily birth and bodily continuance is the Same One responsible for the body waking each morning. This Great Being is not the ego-"I"—it is the <u>Source</u> of ego-"I".

"I" does not give rise to "I". Nor can "I" dissolve "I". The comings and goings of ego-"I" happen naturally and spontaneously within a Condition senior to "I". In other words, ego is an emergent function of something altogether prior to (and transcendent to) ego.

In truth, ego-"I" is the <u>whole</u> bodily (and even total cosmic) process, not merely some private entity (soul) encapsulated within the flesh. "I" is the incarnating process <u>altogether</u> (including the mind and all subtle realms).

Yet even this total body or cosmic continuum is not Identity. The Real Person (Identity) is the Great Being in which the whole body ("I") arises, changes and passes away. The Great One lives and breathes the whole-bodily-cosmic process. As Alan Watts put it, "God is ego-ing."

Ego is real enough—birth and change and death are not illusion—but "I" is only a temporary wave on the timeless ocean. Ego is not the Real Identity. Enlightenment means awakening from the false identification with ego-"I" into awareness of its actual, unqualified condition and identity. This breakthrough process might be difficult, or it might be easy; sudden or gradual.

***

It does not feel scary to fall into dreamless sleep. But it usually feels threatening to come to the brink of ego "death." The advent of ego-"death" (*nirvikalpa samadhi*) is a conscious event—you must witness your own dissolution. You must pass through your own death! Therefore, it requires 1) absolute TRUST to allow the "death" to occur, and 2) the realization that there is no independent position from which to stop the dissolution from proceeding to its end.

You have really got to FEEL your utter dependency on Grace (inherency in God); only then can you let yourself go. You've got to love and trust God enough to be willing to die in God—the source of "I" and everything. Love-surrender all the way through ego-"death" to "rebirth" is the sacrifice enlightenment demands.

I want to make clear that ego will reappear and be operative after the episode of ego-"death." When you reawaken from dreamless (ego-less) sleep, you are not egoless, are you? Similarly, after one consciously passes through the dissolution of ego, ego comes back "online" and it is perfectly functional. But it is also obvious that "I" is not the Real Identity, but only an emergent function or vehicle of Real Identity.

Intuition of the Great One is the ongoing freedom and enjoyment while "I" (the body-mind) continues through all its ordinary and extraordinary states.

Go Gentle into That Good Night

Reality includes maggots. Reality includes germs and vultures and vermin. Without such creatures to consume dead bodies, the biosphere would suffocate in carcasses. Gracefully, the natural order of the universe provides beings that delight in the delicious feast of corpses. The Source, which gives abundant life, also gives abundant death.

Observe the natural world carefully and you will see that you cannot mark sharply where life stops and death begins. The organic environment appears as one dynamic—a blended and interactive whole. The human body, for example, is composed of ever-changing cells that are continually being born and dying and getting recycled in the ongoing process of the organism, until it is necessary for the whole body itself to be recycled.

Life is a process in totality; it is not compartmentalized, but unbroken and unbreakable. What we call life is a seamless continuum that would more accurately be labeled life-death. Death is <u>not</u> the opposite of birth, or of life. Life is not at any instant independent from death. Life and death are inseparable, a single operation. When we say life, we really mean life-death.

"Do not go gentle into that goodnight," penned Dylan Thomas, "Rage, rage, against the dying of the light." With that attitude, you'll go raging, kicking, screaming and begging into that goodnight. But you'll go. Nothing lasts. Everybody, everything goes.

Most humans resist death to the extent that they cannot allow themselves to be completely born. They go around contracted in knots of belly, mind, and heart; recoiled from change and relationship and death—the facts of every life. People refuse life, because they fear that to embrace life is to embrace death. In other words, they fear the truth! To embrace life fully *is* to fully embrace death. But this truth is not popular.

The local and universal process responsible for your birth is also responsible for your death. Reality, Nature, Tao, "Hortense"—whatever you choose to call this process—is not just the condition and process of life, but also of death. Nature is as open to death as to birth. No qualms. No avoidance. No holding back. All is released.

We all fall down. The sacrifice is guaranteed. Even the sun will die. Galaxies, too. The universe itself follows the same course as you and I and the mayfly—*exactly* the same course. There's not a single thing to cling to, because every phenomenon is no more substantial, ultimately, than a dream. Nothing lasts. All parts are recycled within the cosmic and continuing pattern of life-death. And that is solely and precisely the way it IS.

Birth, death and rebirth are the natural and ongoing order of things. Consider this: There have already been uncountable deaths, but all those deaths have not halted or slowed the river of life. Living things keep being born and are as fragile and mortal today as they were a trillion-trillion-trillion deaths ago. Death goes on and on, yet birth goes on and on. This demonstrates a transcendental and all-inclusive condition unscathed by the process of birth and death.

How to Let Go and Die:

- Realize the indivisibility (singularity) of the cosmic process in which the "separate self" appears and disappears.
- <u>Feel</u> and <u>breathe</u> and <u>surrender</u> into this totality.
- Let death happen. Melt into the Heart of the Being. (That is, utterly release the temporary identity into its cosmic matrix.)

Everything that <u>can</u> die <u>will</u> die. That which was never born will shine through, clear and infinite, original and free. Fear may arise during this process of the sacrifice of limited identity. Flow with the truth that there is no turning back, no alternative to the Real. Therefore, let the dissolution occur without withholding a single atom. As the fleeting self and all self-concern vanish, the "void" loses its seeming threat and becomes instead, blissful, Free Radiant Consciousness.

Death is transformation, <u>not</u> annihilation. Death transforms the body-mind, or born personality; it does not touch the uncreated and immutable spirit. To this spirit-source (Buddha Nature, Luminous Emptiness) bodily death is no more threatening than removing a tight boot.

Best of all, we can fully awaken to the deathless, Radiant Consciousness <u>now</u>, even while we manifest in bodily form and its relationships. The summary of all paths to such realization is to abandon limited, false identities, and the final truth is that <u>all</u> identities are limited and false.

This is the Open Secret: There is <u>only</u> God or Indestructible Life.

Death is a spontaneously given event within Immortal Life. May all sentient beings go gently into that goodnight.

ADYASHAKTI

PART SEVEN

Take Heart!

ADYASHAKTI

Taste It for Yourself

> This above all: To thine own self
> be true. And it must follow, as the
> night the day, thou canst not then
> be false to any man. (William
> Shakespeare, *Hamlet,* act 1, sc. 3)

Dog biscuits aren't too bad; kind of dry and bitter. Canned dog food though, is smelly and leaves a grease slick on your tongue.

How do I know these things?

I tasted dog food when I was a kid.

I used to watch my pet dog, Stormy, wolf down his canned food. I loved the mutt and I wondered what his meal tasted like. So, I crouched down beside his food bowl like a member of the pack and I took a bite. I have not forgotten the flavor.

If you want to know the taste of something, you have to taste it for yourself. Otherwise, all you get is hearsay. How can you trust one word of it? Can mere beliefs gratify your heart? Is yours a hunger that can be satisfied by reading menus?

There is no teacher or teaching that you can bank on. You have no "capital" but *your own consciousness in this moment* with which to understand and commune with reality. Therefore, you must settle uncompromisingly into your own truth, apart from all beliefs and conditionings and hopes and fears that tend to push or pull you one way or another. You must come to rest as you *are*, at the ground of your own being.

As the inscription above the ancient Oracle at Delphi advised: *Know thyself.*

All Is Flow

The various qualities of life, with their attendant highs and lows, never cease. These cycles keep rolling on—up and down, 'round and 'round—even in the lives of awakened people. Why shouldn't they? Awakening doesn't *alter* the Tao, the process of the universe, but only our understanding of the Tao.

There will be moments when you feel rather stupid or lazy about your commitment to live happily and freely for the rest of your days; other moments when you're boiling over with energy and creativity; and moments when you feel oceanically peaceful, beatific, Buddha-wise and free. These moments will always come and go. They are examples of the cycling qualities of manifest existence.

Nothing about the worlds is static. All is flow. Likewise, enlightenment is not static. It is not a solid thing, nor a definite state of things. You can't obtain it, or maintain it—for there *is no independent "you"* (distinct from the total flow) to hold on to any exclusive state.

This insight is liberating. One no longer projects upon one's spiritual mentors a frozen condition called "enlightenment," or tries, oneself, to attain such a concrete state of body-mind. As Suzuki Roshi put it: "Strictly speaking, there is no such thing as an enlightened person. There is only enlightened activity."

Because enlightenment is not a state of body-mind, it follows that enlightenment cannot be brought about as a result of changes in the body-mind (changes of state). Rather, enlightenment is the enjoyment of prior (or intrinsic) freedom. You cannot *become* free, as the wise have pointed out, you can only *be* free. This means no matter how much you change (and apparently improve) your state of body and mind and world, you can never "gain" or "own" the power that is already at the heart of the whole process—real freedom and happiness, itself.

You are *already* free and welcome to abide in this prior happy orientation (the vision of Radiant Wholeness) all the while you move through the easeful and stressful moments of your life. In fact, enlightenment is this very presumption of prior freedom and happiness, rather than presuming dilemma and identifying with limited appearances and conditionings.

Enlightenment is an attitude, an understanding, a relationship to everything—*an ongoing Way*. And such enlightenment is nothing special, not apart from life. Life is not a dress rehearsal; a preparation for the glory-to-come; a progressive path toward reality. There is no path, ultimately, but only reality. (How does one "return" to God, when God is not elsewhere?)

Nothing is more than whole. This moment is complete, as is.

This is it, "the full catastrophe," as Zorba the Greek put it. THIS kind of universe. Exactly so. Amazing. Wonderful. Terrible. Blissful.

What can we do about any of it? Take a deep breath. Release our grasp. "Let go with both hands," as Zen teaches. Abandon the principle of all our concerns and all our strategies; or as Krishna puts in the *Bhagavad Gita*, "Abandon all dharmas and resort alone to Me." Thus surrendered, allow everything to come and go in its own way.

Troubles won't disappear. Sickness, old age and death won't disappear. But if we can live in this unreasonably happy way, existence will shine with more and more clarity, and soon we will see for ourselves that reality is fundamentally open, spacious and bright, even while all the possibilities of all the worlds cycle around their source, the Free Sun of the Heart.

ADYASHAKTI

Conclusion: Take Heart!

All that appears only changes and disappears. But the essential nature and condition of all that we love is never threatened. The Basis of all life is immortal (or unborn and undying). The Basis of all is self-radiant being. It is the only "Person," the single Identity or Self of all that appears. The Basis of all is not locatable, but non-local, all-pervading, all-inclusive, complete, prior and absolutely singular.

Reality is never identified. Every identity is un-Real. The Basis of all can never be found, known, remembered, imagined, defined, limited, described or compared. The Only Person is not cognized over and against anything. The Great Person (the Person of all life) can only be intuited and understood. The Radiant Transcendental Being must be accepted (presumed) and <u>directly</u> lived.

Take heart as that one. Take your stand as that one. Live your moments as that one. Be whole. Practice Happiness (Breathe and Feel and Smile).
"Yes" is the Word.
"Amen" is the prayer.

ADYASHAKTI

About the Author

Adyashakti ("Primordial Energy") is the pen name of Mark Canter, who was raised in a tiny farm town—population 400—along the Ohio River in Kentucky, where he and his family were the only Jews in the universe.

Canter is the former Senior Editor of *Men's Health* magazine, and his non-fiction also has appeared in *The Baltimore Sun, San Francisco Chronicle, Denver Post, Miami Herald, St. Petersburg Times, Yoga Journal, Shambhala Sun, Writer's Digest* and other periodicals.

His short fiction has been published nationally and his novels have been translated into Swedish, German, Polish, Dutch, Italian, French, Spanish, Catalan, and Japanese.

Canter holds degrees in journalism and the humanities, with highest honors, and taught for seven years as an adjunct professor in the Florida State University Department of Religion.

"I'm a true romantic," says the author, "and by that I don't mean that I always do something special for my wife on Valentine's Day—although that happens to be the case. I mean that I believe in the Redemptive Power of Love. Every one of my novels expresses the same moral theme: Love (not power) is the only force that can render us fearless.

"That's also a central theme of Romanticism—the artistic, literary, and intellectual movement that began in Europe at the end of the 18th century and peaked in the 19th century, and included the works of Whitman, Emerson, and Thoreau. Another recurring idea that drove the Romantic Era is the revelatory wisdom and beauty of nature. My novels always explore the wonder and wildness, bliss and terror of the human body within the natural world (*Eros* writ with a capital 'E')."

The novels of Mark Canter

Ember from the Sun (science fiction): "Weaves a genuinely magic spell." – Kirkus Reviews

Down to Heaven (action-adventure/romance): "He's the H.R. Haggard of the '90s." – from a Dutch review

Second Nature (science fiction/romance): "Canter once again demonstrates his first-rate ear for dialogue, as well as a knack for nonstop pacing and a thoroughly convincing scientific grounding."– Kirkus Reviews

Orchard of my Eye (science fiction/romance): "Canter weaves together exciting action, tender relationships and plausible science in this thought-provoking thriller." – Kirkus Review

The Bastard (historical fiction/romance): "A compelling what-if story." – Kirkus Reviews

AWAKENING TO THE OBVIOUS

ADYASHAKTI